The Irish Hungarian Guide
to the Domestic Arts

By

Erin O'Brien

Dear Jan~
Thank you for
your support~
Enjoy~
Erin O'Brien
2-2-2012

red giant
books

For Eric and Jessie

Table of Contents

Introduction: The Irish Hungarian

In second grade, I was called into the principal's office wherein a stern man with a handlebar mustache admonished me for wearing jeans to school too frequently.

"Once in a while is fine," he said, sniffing. "But school is not an everyday picnic." The year was 1973.

I trudged home from Taft Elementary in shame, placing one tattered sneaker in front of the other upon the sandstone sidewalks of my overwhelmingly Irish Catholic neighborhood. The girls from St. Luke's School walked in a tight circle on the other side of the street, books clutched to their chests. No redheaded principal in a double-breasted suit would tell those girls to clean up their act. Their pleated skirts flounced along with their shiny bobbed hair. Delicate crosses of gold shone from their throats in holy glory.

They were so close and yet so far, because despite my enviable name, I was not Catholic. I wasn't exactly Protestant either.

"We're Methodists," my mother would say when I asked about religion, although we never went to church save for one Christmas Eve when my father, having had more than a few cups of cheer, decided to take me to Cove United Methodist Church for the evening services. We clumsily arranged ourselves in a pew and commenced singing along to "Oh Holy Night," although "singing" is a generous designation. Neither of us knew the words, which I tried to camouflage by mumbling softly.

Not Dad.

Heads turned and necks craned to see from whence Dad's loud and uneven efforts emanated. Minutes later when the sermon started in earnest, Dad looked around with a smirk and said, "Let's get the hell outta here." We shuffled past the relieved parishioners as their eyes following us from beneath arched brows.

My daily culture was far more Eastern European than Celtic. In addition to my religious ambiguity, I am a patchwork mutt made up of unequal measures of Irish, Hungarian, German, and a splash of French-Canadian. My mother was bred of German and Hungarian immigrants. Although Gram (German) and Gramp Soos (Hungarian) divorced when I was a kid, Gram continued to figure largely in my life. I adored her.

She lived in an apartment on the 25th floor of the ritzy Winton Place on Cleveland's Gold Coast. During my grade school years, Mom worked at the Winton Place as a receptionist, then rental agent, then building manager. Hence, I walked there for my elementary school lunch break to nosh with Mom or Gram, spent untold hours in the indoor/ outdoor pool and had frequent overnight stays in Gram's spacious apartment.

Nearby Greta's Beauty Salon was owned by Greta proper. She was a stunning Austrian woman with a thick accent who, like my Gram, had been married to a Hungarian.

"Come down with me to Greta's while I get my hair cranked up," Gram would say. I'd happily tag along and settle into the seat next to her, licking a Tootsie Pop while spinning myself round and round amid the curlers, dryers and mysterious bottles.

"Greta, I'm telling you," my Gram would say, "he was the worst Hungarian son of a bitch like you never saw."

Greta would fasten a clip to Gram's head, turn to her reflection in the mirror and level her gaze at Gram over her glasses.

"Betty? Vy don't you listen to me?" she'd say, hand on hip, "Ve're better off vizout za sonzabitches." Gram would nod knowingly. Then an elaborate discussion regarding the sexual endeavors and subsequent marital discords of the neighborhood's housefraus would ensue as I listened on, fascinated.

"I heard she's divorcing him," Gram would say.

"Divorsink him?" Greta would say in disbelief. "Honey, she tried to shoot him in za parking lot!"

The O'Brien portion of my name came from a brilliant man I never knew but drew at least fifty percent of my looks from. My great-grandfather was William O'Brien, a Rhodes scholar and decorated chemical engineer who made his name as the first head of research for Akron's Goodyear Tire and Rubber Company in 1914.

My dad was William O'Brien's replicate in image and name, but my father grew up largely under the loose supervision of his maternal grandparents—my great Gram and Gramp Doubler, who worked a potato and sweet corn farm on the banks of the Cuyahoga River. Although they both died when I was very young, my memories of Gram and Gramp Doubler are vivid: Gramp warning me about the "injuns" in the cellar; Gram gently unfolding hand-embroidered hankies and displaying them to me before she'd tell me they were mine to keep.

Hence I grew up eating speck and hominy, slumgullion and sweet corn. My hair grew thick and long as did the most interesting parts of my boyfriends, with their beat-up Fords and Chevys and paper sacks full of Stroh's beer. I read all of Ian Fleming's James Bond books but never touched the Bible. In school, I spit out straight A's with ease, relishing the music that played in my head as I solved one Calculus problem after another. I learned how to smoke, laughed hard and screwed harder.

My innate math and science abilities led me to Ohio

University's college of engineering. I earned my electrical engineering degree at OU in four years and put it to immediate use as a field engineer for Sohio. I worked for them for eight years, collecting adequate paychecks and one husband along the way.

Despite the money and upscale offices, for me the cloak of corporate life was lined with thorns. I started to get bitter around the edges and fall into joyless drinking. The O'Brien was sucking out of me.

I needed to find a new life, something that would accommodate my German technicality, the spot of Frenchie artist, my Irish thirst for whiskey, and my huge Hungarian libido.

I needed a career that would let me fly unfettered, far from electronic gas pumps and car wash designs. *Life is too short for power capacitors and monthly status reports,* I told myself, *you need nice afternoon naps upon a couch outfitted in a comfy blankie nest.* I needed to find a job that would let me give the performance of my choice whenever I wanted. I needed to be able to orchestrate my own convoluted Erin trip through every single day.

Then one day as I sat in front of the box watching Lucille Ball and Tallulah Bankhead settling into coffee at the kitchen dinette, the perfect solution bloomed.

I decided to become a housewife.

Part One: The Happy Household

Housewife

I am a housewife.

I sparkle with brilliance. I dazzle with charisma. I shimmer with wit. I shampoo with Suave.

I have verve, vigor and vim. I have style, flair and élan. I have Comet, Tide and Pledge.

When I exhale, the angels sigh. When I sigh, the angels weep. When I sneeze, Kleenex says, "Bless you."

The fragrance of sugared vanilla wafts from my supple flesh. My lips are lush pillows, the color of pomegranate. My pudendum is a flower of unequaled beauty.

My bra crosses my heart 18 hours a day.

I have vanquished Martha Stewart, June Cleaver and Jane Jetson only to rise from the smoking debris with covered dish in hand.

I dream of fellating Ron Popeil.

When I step into a ballroom, a bevy of tuxedoed dandies rushes to lift me up and carry me high above the crowd before gently setting me upon a bejeweled throne from whence I grin with indulgent affection for my adoring admirers.

When I step into Wal-Mart, a bevy of shopping carts greet me as a blue-vested boy wonder selects one for me before I turn to glide down the aisles, a yellow smiley-face beaming from my sweatshirt.

I have magnificent breasts.

The Domestic Arts

Although I take overblown pride in my title of house-wife, at no time am I inclined to do any actual housework. This is why I defer to the term "Domestic Arts" when it comes to menial household tasks. "Domestic Arts" is replete with delusion. In its realm, I float through an immaculate house, feather duster in hand. Tips and tricks render all things effortless in my fantasy world. Yes Virginia, there really are 101 uses for a cup of vinegar. Toothpaste can remove crayon from walls. Plop a tab of Polident into the toilet bowl and stare deeply into its porcelain depths. Concentrate as hard as you can, babygirl, and when the effervescence subsides, an animated sparkle will glitter from the white white rim.

In this lifetime, I shall relieve a hinge of its squeak with non-stick cooking spray. I shall melt away the tension in a baking soda bath. I shall unscrew a broken light bulb from an electrical socket using a raw potato, and in that simple act, I shall move closer to holiness.

Of course, this level of delusion only gets a girl so far.

Eventually the fog clears and the light dawns. It streams through the streaky windows illuminating plumes of dust motes in the wake of each footfall and drop of limp post-climax forearm upon upholstery.

Black are the days when I must tread through my toppled house of cards and actually clean. I don my frayed Ohio State sweatshirt and turn on the Hoover Bagless Wind-Tunnel, thereby reducing it from an interactive sculpture to a simple vacuum, crass and pedestrian. There is no artistry in a beleaguered scrub brush with bristles bent and dingy. Pick up an ungainly gallon of bleach in one hand and a slovenly jug of ammonia in the other. Simultaneously pour them into a bucket and the resulting fumes can kill you.

Laundry is an emotionally exhausting subject for me as it at once represents the zenith of my craft as well as its prosaic dullness.

Consider the day when I purchased the Kenmore Elite HE3 automatic clothes washer. I was with my husband and daughter. The funding for the purchase was made possible by my mother, who had just given us a generous monetary gift. Despite the surrounding physical and financial participation, I felt singular that day—not alone—but beyond the dilution of others. I was a leader.

It was the fifth and final day of the Sears Laundry Spectacular! I perused the line-up of washers, running my finger over the smooth white enamel of one top-loader after another. Then came the authoritative front-loaders that evoke the Downy-infused air of Laundromats and all their possibilities: generous folding tables, entire wardrobes in one load, and a welcoming beckon to the oversized comforters shunned by residential top-loaders. My pace slowed in front of these majestic statues.

The salesman prattled on, "This model has what they call catalyst cleaning action," he said, accentuating each syllable with both hands, his fingers splayed out as if he were casting a spell. "Injectors actually spray your clothes with detergent in order to saturate ..."

Despite his emphatic delivery, his voice faded into the background as the rest of the stage darkened. It was just the Kenmore Elite HE3 and me in the hot white spotlight. Then a voice rose up between us, a whisper.

This is the Ablution.

I swallowed hard against my dry throat and beheld the 3.8-cubic foot capacity drum and a display that featured seven wash cycles (including delicate, whitest white and hand wash).

The salesman chattered on in the background, "... with an automatic water level feature..."

The variable speed motor with its five spin settings—up to 1050 RPM—and the three-compartment automatic product dispenser, all of it would set me proper upon the yellow brick road to cleanliness. From that moment on, the HE3 was mine and mine alone—make no mistake. If I could, I would draw a heart around HE3 each time I type it.

" ... recommend the optional convenience pedestal for product storage ... "

As if he even had to say one word after "catalyst cleaning action."

The matching HE3 dryer retailed for approximately nine hundred dollars, which conjured the shrewd home economist within. For what is a dryer? Like our Magic Chef 1000-watt 1.1-cubic foot microwave, a dryer is a dullard. The HE3 clothes dryer was no different. Despite its good looks, it was still a one-note straight man standing next to a dazzling comedienne. It's on or it's off. So there's a timer and a temperature control. So what? *These things are splintered bones before a mangy mutt,* the internal thriftmonger persuaded, *surely not worth the $900 price tag.* I veered back to the land of stocky white cubes. The uninspired Kenmore 29-inch super capacity dryer was less than $300. Sold.

"I just saved you $600," I said to my husband, imagining how I might spend said windfall.

Hence when I step into my laundry room, I am not met with two identical eyes worthy of Fitzgerald's Dr. T. J. Eckleburg staring at me from the HE3 washer on the left and the matching HE3 dryer on the right. I am subjected to one of many annoyances that make up the hellish task of doing the laundry: the visual inequity of the grand HE3 next to that blockhead of a dryer. Behold the price of compromise.

I do not fault the HE3 for the fundamental truth that is the laundry. Instead, I would apologize to it for the inequity of its mate (for this was a pre-arranged marriage), for stuffing it with stained sheets, soiled underwear, odiferous socks and sweaty gym clothing. The cracked plastic laundry baskets, the perfumed chemicals, the metal snaps and accoutrements that punish the stainless steel washer drum, baiting its limited lifetime warranty—all of it is an assault to this, the Auguste Rodin of household appliances.

Doing the laundry actually sullies my washer.

But just like Cleveland's *The Thinker*, (which is different from all the other monumental casts of Rodin's number one dude on account of having its nether region and feet blown to bits in 1970 by a homemade bomb, but being a true Clevelander, our *Thinker* got right back up and settled into his usual spot in front of the Cleveland Museum of Art and has been there ever since—a bunch of candy-ass vandals don't run you down in a town like this), the HE3 stoically accepts its fate, soaking, washing and spinning so quietly that I am often obliged to step into the laundry room in order to verify its operation while muttering to myself, "Did I push start? Goddamnit anyway..." only to find the HE3 answering my every query, silently segueing from wash to drain to spin while refusing to draw attention to its obvious magnificence.

My washer is the placid eye in a storm that starts with our filthy human emanations and ends with an unruly pile of laundered fabric, waiting for the monotonous folding. Hence, while I would be content to sip a deep Burgundy and watch the HE3 operate for hours on end, I still hate doing the laundry.

Aversions can sometimes have windfalls of their own.

My splendid king returned home from work one day with a hangar of clothing draped over his arm. From this he produced a work shirt that I had not seen before. He slipped it on. There was a name patch over his heart. "Eric," it said.

"What's all this?" I asked.

He explained that the uniform was part of the new job he had accepted within the company.

"Oh perfect!" I said, with an inflection that implied the situation was anything but.

"What's the problem?" he asked.

"The shirt has a name patch," I lamented. "A name patch for chrissake!"

"So?"

"So!" I said incredulously. "What about my fantasies starring guys in chinos and work shirts with embroidered name patches?"

"So I'm a fantasy come true?"

"No," I said, infuriated. "You're you. You're my husband."

"I can leave the shirt on while we screw."

"I don't want you to leave the shirt on while we screw. I don't want to think of you in a shirt with a name patch. I am wholly entitled to fantasize about any man I want. Now the vision of you in the name patch shirt ruins the whole guy-in-a-name-patch-shirt fantasy."

He considered this for a moment. "Want me to borrow a shirt from one of the other guys at work?"

"Why?" I asked.

"It'll have a different name."

"That isn't the point," I said. "It will still have you inside of it."

"There is one other thing about my new work clothes," he said.

"Oh?"

"They come with a service."

"A service?" I asked.

"A laundering service," he said. "The service will wash all my work clothes." I stood before him blinking.

When the joyous revelation sunk in, I dropped to my knees in order to fellate him.

Prelude to a Cold Meatloaf Sandwich

The first time I went to my husband's home before we were married, I did exactly what a new girlfriend is supposed to do: I promptly inspected the interior of his refrigerator. It housed a case of Pabst beer (cans), a case of Pepsi (also cans), a one-gallon pitcher of iced-tea (reconstituted from powder that was housed in a 53-ounce canister) and the largest package of individually wrapped American cheese slices I have ever seen.

"Nice," I said, eyeing the shelves.

The remainder of the house matched the refrigerator in design as well as spirit. Two of the bedrooms contained a bed and a nightstand each. The third bedroom was devoid of all furniture. Instead, the entire floor was lined with open cardboard boxes, each filled with paperback books (similarly, one kitchen cabinet was dedicated to the hallowed shot glass collection). There were exactly two decorative items on the walls of the house: a Cleveland Browns Christmas tree ornament that hung from a nail above the couch and, in one of the spare bedrooms, a beach towel that was tacked to the wall and featured a distorted circa 1980 Cleveland skyline on which the "fun" venues such as Muni Stadium and the Flats were disproportionately larger than say, the National City Bank building.

On my second visit, the books, beds, shot glasses, ornament, etc. were the same as they were the first time. The refrigerator still contained the Pabst, Pepsi, iced-tea and cheese. But there were two new items in the Amana: a case of Bud Light and a case of Diet Pepsi, my two preferred brands of carbonated beverage.

Standing in the chilly glow of his refrigerator, I fell in love with Eric Nowjack precisely at that moment.

After a year of courtship and a year of engagement, we purchased a circa-1967 classic suburban split-level home on Cleveland's south side that I often refer to as being "Brady Bunch approved." I accepted the shot glass collection (in part), the Browns ornament (for annual yule-tide display), and the paperbacks (dispatched to the attic). He also owned four plastic tumblers, each of which was festooned with a piece of felt fashioned after a golf green along with a marking flag indicating where the imaginary hole would be. This embellishment was in the interstitial space between the interior and exterior of the tumbler that presumably rendered it "insulated."

"I will not have those in my new house," I said of the golf-tumblers.

My groom exhaled flatly and picked up the phone to call my future mother-in-law. He told her that her future daughter-in-law had rejected the set of tumblers that she had given him for his birthday three years ago and did she want them back or should he go ahead and put them in the Goodwill pile? I listened on as my supple brunette tendrils turned to snakes and tiny flames flared from my nostrils. This would require more behavior correction than I had originally estimated.

I married him anyway.

Although the 53-ounce Nestea container became a change pot (housed on the floor of my husband's closet), the hideous iced tea pitcher did not make the cut (it was plastic and the color of dubious urine), nor did the giant package of cheese slices. We would do processed American cheese food my way: If you want a cheeseburger, I espoused, you slice a slab of Velveeta off the two-pound brick, by God!

The arrangement by which I was reared worked out well enough until our daughter arrived on the scene in 1997 and grew into a kid. Kids require individually wrapped American cheese slices. It is a law. Fortunately by that time, Velveeta had begun packaging the staple of my youth in single-serve slices. Even I had to admit they were infinitely easier to manage than the two-pound brick, which got sticky and icky right around the halfway mark. A perfect compromise was born.

Square slices of individually wrapped Velveeta cheese are conducive to sandwiches made with Wonder Bread and for folding into fourths for application onto four saltine crackers. Applying a Velveeta cheese square to a cheese-burger, however, is ridden with angst. What about those floppy corners hanging out?

My solution to this dilemma (which I did not have with the brick due to its dimensions—one slice fit a burger perfectly) is to fold each of the four corners inward and squish them until they stick. I thusly transform the cheese square into a cheese octagon with four longish sides and four shortish sides. The result approximates a circle that fits nicely betwixt patty and bun.

Although I have been known to use Velveeta cheese in the composition of a sandwich, I much prefer an earthier experience. A sandwich should say something about who you are. Certainly I enjoy a simple ham on rye, but a stretchy pita slathered with hummus, sprinkled with finely diced green pepper, cucumber and pickled turnips, then rolled into a to-go lunch has that certain *je-ne-sais-pas* that eludes a turkey club wrap.

The ever-present brick of Velveeta of my youth notwithstanding, I began developing those permanent sandwich preferences in the early 1980s when I worked bussing and waiting tables during summer breaks. During that time period, I established deep emotional roots in the connection between my professional and sandwich eating endeavors.

The Marius restaurant boasted a beautiful dining room on Lake Erie in the once opulent and famous Lake Shore Hotel, which remains one of the most incredible examples of Art Deco architecture in Northeast Ohio. The Lake Shore opened in 1929. Fifty-one years later, I started working there in my black bow tie and vest. I was just 15 years old, but I was developing a chapter on experience like no other in my life.

The last remnants of Cleveland's Mafia drank and laughed in the sequestered bar, The Flying Dutchman, which was named after Marius, the Dutch proprietor. Marius liked me and indicated as much by referring to me as "little shit-ass," a term of endearment for him.

"Turn that four-top, you little shit-ass!" he'd yell in his thick Dutch accent, made even more gravelly by the ever-present Pall Mall. The same voice would turn to velvet when a quartet of beautiful woman stepped into the dining room for lunch.

"Ladies, today's beef medallions are nearly as perfect as you," he'd say, evoking their delighted titters (the same results when Marius repeated the line verbatim to a slow-moving group of blue-haired members of the Ladies' Auxiliary). He was devastatingly attractive, swarthy, tall and barrel-chested with a thick shock of silver hair.

Similarly, the tuxedoed waiters were smooth gentlemen on the floor and filthy-mouthed rogues in the kitchen and back pantry. This was at a time when "sexual" and "harassment" were just two words that had nothing in common, so the waiters had no qualms drawing attention to their favorite part of my anatomy. They dubbed me the "bus-tit." After all, busboy wasn't exactly right. The hard waitresses were jealous of those same attributes and treated me with guarded toleration or disdain. There were the odd exceptions.

Jill was a rail-thin brunette who would lean against the backroom wall clutching herself with her right arm and holding a cigarette an inch from her lips with her left hand. She'd stare off at some unseen starlight with a misty look.

"Someday, kid," she'd say to me, then suck deeply from her Winston and exhale thoughtfully, "I'm gonna make it in Nashville." Then she'd quietly hum/sing a few notes until one of us was obliged to attend to a waiting deuce or party of six.

I spent hours folding crisp linen napkins at the back table with the other wait staff, smoke curling from our cigarettes that were propped in the ashtray in the center of the table. I learned the nuances of the term "bar back" and how to prepare a tableside cooking cart for Marius's "famous" Caesar Salad, Steak Diane, or one of the flambéed desserts. Then I'd wheel it out onto the main floor and stand next to him, silently assisting while he charmed diners over sautéing Bananas Foster.

"I know what you like!" he'd say to his captivated audience as the fragrant brown sugar/butter sauce made my mouth water. Then he'd spoon the hot bananas and sauce over scoops of vanilla ice cream that were waiting in gleaming wine goblets and place them on the table with a flourish. I'd roll the cart into the back for clean up, but not before lapping up a clandestine spoonful of syrup from the bottom of the pan. Pure heaven, that.

The kitchen was always 100 degrees or hotter. Save for Doreen the salad lady, the kitchen staff was terrifying. Nico the Greek cook constantly yelled and swore, his big afro-style hair bobbing back and forth. He drank ouzo from a tumbler he'd set on the steam table where it would get hot as hell. Sometime he threw trays.

"Goddamnnit!" Nico's voice would boom through the kitchen as a cocktail tray sailed overhead.

Mike the dishwasher loved me.

"I love you Erin O'Brien," he'd say as I set down a tray for him to unload. He had a pet python he kept in the trunk of his "beater."

"Hey Erin O'Brien, you want to meet Chaz?"

"Um, no thanks, Mike. Gotta stock the bar glasses. Gotta ice the bar."

Eventually my excuses wore out and, near the end of

what had been a busy Saturday night, I broke down and accepted Mike's invitation to say hello to his pet snake.

We stood in the parking lot, the balmy lake breeze swirling around us. Mike the dishwasher opened his trunk, revealing Chaz, who remained in his thick coil, indifferent to the proceedings. I have never been afraid of snakes, so I was not intimidated. However, when I turned to tell Mike the dishwasher how attractive Chaz was only to see that Mike had unleashed a much more personal snake that he was vigorously stroking, that repelled me.

"I love you Erin O'Brien," he said.

Another girl might have been scared or felt threatened. Another girl might have been angry. I felt none of that. My repulsion stemmed from the fact that I was not complicit in the act. That felt wrong. A girl should have options.

"I better get back in there," I said, stepping backward.

I rushed back to the steamy kitchen. The back door opened right next to Doreen's station. Donna Summer's voice blared from her tinny radio as Doreen sang along.

"She Works Hard for the Money!" she crooned, pointing at me as I hurried out to the dining room and as far from Mike as I could get.

Such was my introduction into the professional world.

At the end of the night, I was always exhausted and

sweaty. My feet would hurt. But along with all of that came satisfaction in the $20 or $30 in tips that lined my pocket as I trudged home.

Dad would be watching *The Tonight Show* with Johnny Carson, his elbow propped on the armrest of the couch, his fist balled up between his chin and chest. I'd flop down next to him.

"Hi Dad."

"Hey Skeeziks."

After a few minutes of the monologue or Stump the Band or Carnac the Magnificent, I'd feel a slight tickle on my baby toe and glance over to see that it was just Dad executing one of his favorite Dad tricks: he would take his Stanley measuring tape (which he always had either clipped to the front pocket of his jeans or next to him atop the side table along with his whiskey and water) and slowly unfurl it so the metal tape would remain stiff. He would carefully and silently extend it until he could tease me or whoever was nearby with the tip by tapping their Diet Pepsi can (simple) or tugging their shirt pocket (intermediate) or pushing a potato chip out of the bowl at their elbow (advanced).

"D-a-ad!" I'd say and he would hissle and giggle and let the metal tape measure snap back into its sheath before setting it back on the side table and then he'd hissle some more while I made *tsk* noises.

Finally he'd ask, "Want a green bean sandwich?"

"That'd be great."

We never made a green bean sandwich with two pieces of bread. It was always one piece folded over and eaten in the manner of a hotdog. First, we'd slather a piece of bagged bread with a dollop of sour cream (cream cheese will do in a pinch, as will cottage cheese). Then we'd add a scant handful of leftover cooked green beans (cold—right from the fridge and they had to have been fresh—not canned) and a few shakes of hot sauce. Fold the whole thing over and there you go.

Having made the offer, Dad would go into the kitchen and emerge with two folded green bean sandwiches and his refreshed whiskey and water.

"Here you go," he'd say, already chewing a bite of his sandwich and proffering the other to me. In Mom's absence, we were free from plates and napkins. We'd scarf down our respective sandwiches in two or three bites. Ten seconds after the last swallow one of us would say, "You want another?"

"You having another?"

"If you're having another, then I'll have another."

"Okay, let's have another."

For Dad and Johnny Carson and me, the only thing that would trump a green bean sandwich was the implication of leftover meatloaf and the *raison d'être*: a great cold meatloaf sandwich.

1. Unwrap a two-or three-pound package of meatloaf mix (like your mom used to buy: that three-different-ground-meats thing in the butcher case, usually 1/3 beef, 1/3 pork and 1/3 veal) and plop it into a bowl.

2. Add a good shake of dry parsley, lots of salt and pepper, two or three squarshy shots of ketchup, a couple of shakes of Worcestershire sauce, a handful or so of dry bread crumbs and one very finely chopped medium-to-large yellow onion.

3. Bask in a surge of overconfidence and tell self, "self, you have made this meatloaf so many times that checking the recipe Mom typed out for you and put in a mini three-ring notebook when you got your first apartment is redundant."

4. Get your damn hands in there and mix it up (use disposable latex gloves if you don't want to get icky meat stuff under your fingernails).

5. Add more ketchup if it seems too dry and more breadcrumbs if it seems too blucky. (You just sort of have to know what constitutes too dry or too blucky. If you

figured out squarshy from step 2, you're on the scene.)

6. Plop resulting mixture onto a large piece of heavy duty foil (the duty of which is not nearly as heavy as it used to be, just ask your mom) and form it into a loaf.

7. Discard gloves. Wash hands.

8. Wrap loaf up tightly in tinfoil so it looks like a giant silver turd.

9. Put loaf in freezer.

10. Sit down and pop a beer. Pour it into the insulated golf-theme tumbler that is exactly like the ones your mother-in-law bought for your husband before you knew him and that you made him get rid of when you got married and replaced sixteen years later—one year after your mother-in-law suddenly died—via eBay for much more money than they were worth in a literal sense and not nearly as much money as they were worth in an emotional sense.

11. Mid-sip, realize you forgot to put the egg in the meatloaf.

12. Engage in futile argument with self over importance of the addition of beaten egg to meatloaf.

13. Simultaneously win and lose argument

14. Say "aw shit" and let out a big sigh.

15. Retrieve meatloaf from freezer.

16. Say "aw shit" again when you look at the mixing bowl full of soapy water in the sink.

17. Wash and dry bowl.

18. Open meatloaf and plop into bowl.

19. Beat and add one egg.

20. Get out another pair of gloves.

21. Get your damn hands in there and mix in the egg, while noting how cold that meatloaf has gotten even though it was only in the freezer for steps 9 through 15.

22. Not wanting to use yet another pair of gloves, remove only the left-hand one and retrieve meatloaf recipe Mom wrote out for you 20 years ago and make sure you haven't forgotten anything else.

23. Add some oregano and basil per Mom's recipe.

24. Using only the one hand that remains in a glove, mix that into the meatloaf as best you can.

25. Plop meatloaf back onto the tinfoil you used previously.

26. Realize that the used tinfoil is too crinkly to reuse, no doubt due to the decreased heaviness in the assertion "heavy duty" on the box as noted in step 6.

27. Take off other glove and say "goddamnit" as the memory of a big Greek man with a bobbing afro dances through the back of your mind.

28. Fumble around in the impossible plastic-bag-and-Saran Wrap drawer and retrieve not-as-heavy-duty-as-it-used-to-be tinfoil.

29. Swear when it doesn't tear properly.

30. Assign improper tearing to tinfoil dispenser box

instead of operator error.

31. Place torn piece of tinfoil upon microwave for future yet-to-be-determined use.

32. Tear off another piece of tinfoil.

33. Internally refuse to use another pair of gloves.

34. Using bare hands, form meatloaf into a loaf.

35. Wash hands, making sure to get icky meat stuff out from under fingernails.

36. Put meatloaf in freezer.

37. Finish the beer you poured in step 10.

38. Empty the dishwasher, clip the $1-off coupon for soy milk, change the sheets, pay the mortgage, buy soy milk while forgetting to use the coupon, measure for new bathroom curtains using the Stanley measuring tape your Dad unclipped from his pocket before going to the ER for chest pains that would end abruptly with a fatal aortic dissection, make love, cry, laugh, fade and shine for a few weeks.

39. Wake up one day and realize there is nothing for dinner.

40. Remember frozen meatloaf.

41. Forget to take meatloaf out of freezer to thaw.

42. With only step 40 in mind (and, naturally, not step 41), conduct day as if dinner will be homemade meatloaf.

43. Realize planned dinner is frozen solid.

44. Spend eighteen seconds deciding whether or not

to schlep to the store, amass dinner ingredients and cook dinner.

45. Delude self into believing sufficient time does not exist between present time and dinnertime to complete step 44.

46. Read, employ marital aid or nap until 25 minutes before dinner.

47. Order pizza from the two mean Italian ladies at the corner pizza joint who make great pizza despite meanness.

48. Take meatloaf out of freezer for tomorrow's dinner.

49. Live another 23 hours or so.

50. Preheat oven to 350 degrees.

51. Place unwrapped meatloaf in shallow baking pan with 1/2" of water.

52. Bake uncovered for about an hour and a half.

53. Make some mashed potatoes and salad while the meatloaf is baking.

54. Open a five-dollar bottle of wine.

55. Knowing that this is nothing more than an obligatory stop on your quest for a great cold meatloaf sandwich, consume meatloaf (deluged with A1 Steak Sauce if desired), potatoes, salad, and wine with family.

56. Refrigerate leftover meatloaf.

57. Live another 18 hours or so in sublime anticipa-

tion of forthcoming lunch.

58. Remove cold meatloaf from fridge and precisely cut one or two slices, depending on cross-sectional area of meatloaf and bread.

59. Marvel at how much easier it is to cut cold meatloaf than hot meatloaf.

60. Lightly toast two pieces of bread.

61. Slather one or both pieces of toast with mayonnaise.

62. Build sandwich: toast, meatloaf, shake of salt, shake of Tabasco, lettuce, mayonnaise-slathered toast.

63. Cut sandwich in half and part the halves such that satisfying cross section of sandwich is viewable.

64. Put a handful of Ruffles on plate, along with a pickle spear.

65. Turn on some Van Morrison, set plate on kitchen table.

66. Sit down.

67. Smile and consider sandwich.

68. Bite sandwich.

69. Inflate with breath as your shoulder blades unfurl into silken wings.

Vita-Mixing the Healthy and Delicious Way

"Your total cholesterol is 360," announced my doctor, emphatically adding that this was a matter of some concern. It was 1992 and I had been married less than a month. I was 28.

I have no intention of droning on about the nutritional, physical and medicinal measures I've taken in order to address my cholesterol situation over the years. The reason that disclosure is pertinent to these pages is that my staggering cholesterol level led me down many paths, including one that ended with yet another of my kitchen's mysterious and spectacular amenities: the Vita-Mix Maxi 4000.

After learning that I had Crisco extruding through my veins, I spent hours on the couch, a Marlboro Light in my right hand and any given diet or health tome that I'd borrowed from the library in my left. I'd pause to sip my whiskey and soda, blow a plume of smoke into the ether of our family room and comment on my reading.

"Saturated fat," I'd say to my husband. "Looks like it's goodbye goose liver and onion sandwiches. Bacon? I'm supposed to live without bacon? And butter as well?. Well then, I guess we'll see if everything really is better with Blue Bonnet on it." Trans fats? Who'd ever heard of trans fats?

Then one day the mail delivered unto me a flyer from the good people of the Vita-Mix Corporation. They touted their product as a "total juicer" that could also grind grain into flour and knead bread dough. The Maxi 4000 was the quintessential health food accessory that cleaned itself to boot.

"Now you can control your nutritional and caloric intake," claimed the promotional material. "Double your fiber. Cut sugar and sodium by 50 percent. Achieve the Vita-Mix Optimum Health Lifestyle!" All of this as well as untold dollar savings were to be had within the confines of the 72-ounce carafe with its Action Dome lid and pressurized spigot.

I reported my findings to my husband, particularly the wonders of the Vita-Mix's patented Impact Lever.

"How do you turn an entire head of cabbage into a delicious bowl of pineapple coleslaw in less than five seconds?" I said to him.

"Dunno," he replied from behind the sports section.

"Why, by instantaneously reversing the direction of the Vita-Mix's hammermill blades of course!" I said, then explained that doing so will turn the blades into vicious culinary battering rams as they collide head-on with the cabbage bits, which are swirling like a Texas twister courtesy of the 24,000-RPM motor.

But this feat cannot be achieved by some vapid mechanical reversal. No slowing and restarting of gears, no dullard processing suited for the general mediocrity can reverse the hammermill blade rotation instantaneously. In order to achieve pineapple coleslaw heaven, the Maxi 4000 must be infinitely more advanced, I told my husband (although neither of us would ever eat anything resembling pineapple coleslaw unless under duress, perhaps if a watchful aunt produced same and was carefully monitoring who took a spoonful from the buffet at Cousin Jenny's birthday party and who subsequently consumed that spoonful and their corresponding reaction). Accomplishing this goal was made possible via the Vita-Mix's spring loaded Impact Lever. One flick and the whirring blades immediately change direction because that little red switch just *reversed the magnetic polarity of the motor's windings!*

"How fucking brilliant is that?" I posed in pure wonderment. My husband did not answer. The Vita-Mix retailed for $495.

"Five hundred bucks," I said. "Holy shit!" and thus ended my dream of whipping myself into a Galatea worthy of Euell Gibbons—or so I thought.

Some months later, on December 25, 1994, after all the

gifts were open and that portion of the holiday proceedings was apparently over, my dearly beloved presented me with a huge box. It was of course, my coveted Vita-Mix Maxi 4000. When I lifted the burnished stainless steel carafe from the packaging and placed it upon the retro-style one-horsepower motor base, the vision took my breath away. In another reality, I might have genuflected before it.

I pawed through the recipe book in search of a concoction for my maiden voyage. I found it on page 15: Tomato Onion Cheese Soup, which was insipid and unworthy of the marvel before me, but it would have to do. It was the only recipe for which I had all of the ingredients—sort of. So I'd use Velveeta instead of cheddar and canned tomatoes would do fine over fresh. Who could wait to boil water? Hot tap would have to do. You really don't need that tomato paste and why not just go ahead and use a whole onion instead of a measly quarter? I hastily piled all of it into the carafe and turned that mother on to high.

The kitchen filled with roaring thunder as the ingredients took flight, becoming a barely contained cyclone that splashed out of the top of the Action Dome and sloshed over Formica and linoleum before settling into a high-speed whir. The whole affair vibrated with life. I steadied it with my hands for fear the Maxi 4000 might shimmy across the counter and ravage the mild-mannered toaster.

The red candy-like Impact Lever gleamed from the

motor base. The recipe did not call for its employ, but then again, the recipe didn't call for the tablespoon of salt I'd added either. I placed my trembling finger upon the lever, took a moment to savor the anticipation, and pushed that mother down.

A loud CRACK snapped through the kitchen as a blue-white flash ignited from beneath the roaring machine.

"AAHH!" I belted and waited for the eruption of flames and smoke. They never came. Instead, the Vita-Mix politely, albeit loudly, continued operation in the reverse direction. My husband and I looked at each other, then back at the Vita-Mix. I flicked the switch again, another snap and electrical flash, then forward swirling. My face split into a wide grin. This machine didn't just operate, it performed. I flicked the Impact Lever again. And again and again. I threw my head back in maniacal laughter. This was no silly little appliance, I thought, this was an industrial-strength power tool for the mightiest of housewives!

"If I ever ice you, Nowjack," I yelled over the din, preferring to use his surname at such moments, "I'm using this Maxi 4000 to get rid of your body. I'll just process you one chunk at a time and pour you down the sink."

"You think that thing will process bone?" he said as I turned off the machine, making his "bone" an inadvertently loud trumpet in the sudden quiet. I poured us each a taster cup of soup. It was blood red and thick as a milkshake.

"The brochure said it'll grind wood into dust," I said and took a sip of our first Vita-Mix creation. I immediately grimaced at the pure saltiness of it, then hunched over the sink and spit it out. "Good God!" I said, heaving. Despite my reaction, my husband tried his anyway.

"Think I'd taste this salty?" he said.

I took his cup and poured out the contents then did the same with what was left in the carafe. We watched the red sludge ooze down the drain. "You'd go down just like that," I said.

"What part would you start with?" he asked.

"Not sure," I said, "maybe a knee."

"Sounds good on paper," he said, "but the prep work would be a real mess."

"True," I conceded.

"For instance," he said, "I don't think you could fit my skull in there."

"Good point," I said. "And then there's all that pesky DNA evidence."

"Maybe you'd better start with something simple," he said.

"What?" I said. "Wasn't this Velveeta Tomato Surprise simple enough for you?

"A machine like this," he said nodding towards the shining tower that was the Vita-Mix, "deserves something with a little inspiration."

###

And from the good earth sprouted the green, green maize. And it did blossom and man learned that its fruit was sweet for the soul and rich for the body. There was the glory of buttered corn, of bread made from corn, of corn on the cob. But woman from whence life is born knew a loftier end was to be had. With this she sets forth and seeks this goal.

In her Mini chariot delivered unto her from the house of Cooper she does travel from the land of developments and parks and malls to the domains of fields and farms and pastures. Therein she finds a wayside stand and trades five clams for 12 ears.

"Behold this golden gift!" she cries.

Shucks the corn, does she, whilst biting her lip against the urge to take His Name in vain as the papery skin resists her honest efforts and strands of silken fiber do stick to her naked, sweat-sheathed legs in the thick hot air. "Let not the Devil's words come into thine," she repeats whilst her strong hands crack stub of stalk from cob.

Into a great pot she does place the corn with two inches of good fresh water and to a boil, she brings this.

Whilst the corn does simmer, covered, for 25 minutes, she cries heavy tears as she dices two medium yellow onions, then sets them aside, thankful.

Into a heavy pot, worthy of stews to feed men that work the land, with muscles bulging, with dungarees filthy from sweat and toil that bind across their virile loins, she does place six slices of finely diced raw bacon and she does sauté them until they are crispy perfect bits.

She removes the pieces of swine with a slotted spoon and sets them aside. Into the fat rendered from the low creature, she adds four tablespoons of good butter. And it does melt over a medium heat. And into the good rich fat, she sends aloft the diced onions and cooks them until they succumb to a mellow translucence.

Six medium potatoes, with skin red and meat white, pulled from the earth, then delivered to her via a market super, she does command. And as she presses them unto her ample, heaving bosom, she knows deep, deep, deep, so deep inside of her these are no lowly roots, but instead they are her blessed vehicle, and peel them she does. And cube them, she does. And unite them with the rendered fat and onion, she does. Over this, pours she, one or two cups of fine chicken broth, enough to just cover the blessed spuds.

To a glorious simmer, this is brought!

She pours into her coarse goblet a measure of wine from the kitchen skin, to give her strength with which to drain the corn and cool it in water. She is good, this woman, and knows that she may savor one ear to nourish her bountiful flesh so she may well complete the daily tasks before her. And she does raise one on high to admire it, the firm texture and size of it, verifying its hefty girth with her palm and gently moving her lips along the length of it, caressing it with a chaste kiss before sinking her teeth into the tender kernels. Sighs with intense satisfaction, does she.

Eleven ears remain, now cooled enough to handle. With a blade sharp, she shears from them the would-be seeds that will not find homes in the good earth. At the mercy of her knife, the kernels fall off in sheets from the cobs, but it is not enough for her. She pours more wine from the skin and takes each stripped ear and scrapes it heartily with a duller blade, extracting every drop of thick white nectar that seeps from where the rows of seed were laid open. It pools, pearly and sweet in the bottom of her bowl amid the glistening yellow nibs.

And all of the freed kernels and all of the cob scrapings and milk squeezed from those sturdy rods go into the pot with the onions and potatoes. And this simmers for a scant handful of minutes until the potatoes are cooked and all flavors are married.

Then it is time for rest and cooling. She places the pot into the cold box of Amana and empties the last of the wine into her goblet.

And the great pot does cool.

Her shaking hand hovers over the devilish Accent, but only for a moment for she knows this red and virgin-white shaker that *Wakes Up Food Flavor!* is nothing more than MSG. She leaps over that temptation and lets her hand drop to the good salt of the earth. She heaves a great sigh of relief and shakes this heartily into the pot, and follows with pepper.

Into the pot she does pour one cup of wholesome milk, collected by young fertile mothers in their comely skirts from the udders of gentle blinking cows.

Lastly, the good woman approaches the mixer of Vita, her balled fist at her chest holding the welling reverence and awe within her. For so palpable are these thrumming emotions that she fears they might verily spill out upon the rough-hewn floorboards, taking her soul with her.

Into the glorious shining vessel she does ladle two cups of her humble corn porridge. For a moment she pauses to behold the gleaming vision before her. And with the power given her, she lays hands upon the mixer of Vita, releasing the howling roar of Divinity to the enlightened space around her.

The porridge swirls into a thickener true, but to ensure its grace and purity, the woman, with eyebrow arched, looks past her tendrils cascading over shoulder right, then turns cheek and looks over shoulder left, to ensure no evil walks with her.

Throw the shining lever of impact does she!

The vessel of Vita does crack in thunder and snap in lightening. The woman throws the lever of impact again and again, her passion rising within her until finally she throws back her head in ecstasy as a tear squeezes from her eye and a gasp overcomes her. Succumbs, does she, to a tiny crumple as the calm quiet fills her simple kitchen. Her heat falls. Her breath quiets. Her glory shines.

Recovered, she pours the thickened porridge into the great pot and heats it again, slowly as not to curdle the milk and as to revel in the peaceful dénouement.

Into bowls she does ladle the thick hot soup, which she then sprinkles with the reserved bits of crispy bacon.

She drops to her knees and offers the bowl to the heavens. "Behold," she whispers, "this divine corn chowder."

The Properly Accessorized Kitchen

I select every kitchen gadget and accessory based not only on its technical specifications, but also on its physical appearance and my emotional connection to it. For instance, my lobster claw crackers are fire engine red and shaped like lobster claws, thereby making the instructions for use inherent in the design–a brilliant and economical achievement. In addition, the handle of my mini-whisk is shaped like an egg. But instead of a simple ovoid blob, this egg has feet and a tiny chicken face that bears an expression of sadness and dissatisfaction, as if it is judging me when whisk meets yolk. Hence, in this simple and effective device, there is somehow room for social commentary as well as an unexpected point of view–stunning. I also own a salt and pepper set that are two amputated feet with painted toenails. The shakers closely resemble my feet, although they sport only one color of polish versus the revolving rainbow I apply to my own toesies. The set was gifted to me by my freshman college roommate who, whenever it is appropriate, still enjoys recollecting my daily awakening back at McKinnon Hall on the South Green of Ohio University as I slid from the bunk above her. First was the appearance of my terrible feetsies, she'll report, followed by the vee of my black undies and then finally my naked breasts. So the darling ceramic feet not only sprinkle the two most basic kitchen seasonings, they also deliver a subtle dusting of salad-day nostalgia.

But what might a garlic press echo?

My garlic press is completely utilitarian. Unlike the foot shakers, lobster claw cracker and mini-whisk, it has no cute embellishments or cleverly shaped handles. (I do own a garlic roaster that is shaped like a head of garlic, but it failed to garner my adoration, [which might admittedly have to do with my failure to properly employ it]. It has been dispatched to the Cabinet of No Return along with a collection of unattractive vases, candles, mason jars, and an inexplicable set of six tiny painted wood Easter eggs still in the display box.) Although subtle in form, my garlic press is perhaps the most emotionally complex gadget in the drawer.

It is constructed of stainless steel so highly polished that I can use it to check my teeth for unwanted bits of oregano or poppy seeds. (I detest poppy seeds and have never once used them in cooking, but since they are the gold standard for items lodged betwixt teeth, I've included them in the preceding description.) Moreover, since stainless steel removes garlic odor from the skin, I worry the press in my hands under running water after handling the garlic as a matter of hygiene for myself as well as the gadget. Since the curvy design of the press begs to be handled, it all culminates to a nearly perfect garlic crushing experience replete with power: The universe is in my hand and at my command.

That said, I am deeply ambivalent towards my garlic press on a sexual level. On one hand, it echoes the thrilling njoy Pure Wand, which is a curved eight-inch affair that features a one-inch sphere on one end and a hefty one and a half-inch ball on the other. It weighs over one and a half-pounds and is constructed of the finest 316-grade surgical stainless steel, which was more or less the deciding factor in its purchase. If the material used to construct the njoy Pure Wand is worthy of your Aunt Ginger's hip replacement, it's surely worthy of my pudendum.

The resulting device is so efficacious that, should I ever be elected President of the United States, my first order of business will be to send every adult American woman an njoy Pure Wand. Believe me, the state of the Union will improve remarkably within a half hour. To hell with your economic incentive checks, stimulus bills and recovery plans.

Savory garlic to my right, joyous orgasms to my left: wherein lies the conundrum?

There is another curvy device fashioned from shiny steel that bears an uncanny resemblance to my garlic press and is regularly inserted into vaginas daily from coast to coast. Its appearance is usually preceded by the donning of a medical examination gown, the guidance of feet into stirrups, and the impossible command to "Relax." Oh really? The mere mention of the word speculum sends most women (myself included) running for the nearest tavern.

Hence, when I hold this common kitchen gadget in my hand, so benign and familiar, I find myself at once filled with the trepidation of the gynecologist's waiting room as well as the heady recollections of my last session with my favorite marital aid. I blink at the press beneath a knitted brow and exhale.

"What did I say I was making again, honey?"

If we're going to start with the garlic, let's start with the garlic. I hope I don't need to say this, but you never know: STEP AWAY from the dehydrated garlic, the granulated garlic or (god help us) that pre-minced garlic in a jar. As for those well-behaved uniform heads of garlic stacked in a mesh sock, you're kidding me, right?

You want a big gnarly head of garlic from the produce market where they have it in real bins (or even a cardboard box) and not in those bins that are trumped up to look like they just got unloaded from the back of the farmer's truck but in fact are totally lame, specifically manufactured with a false bottom thereby making not so many heads of garlic look like a whole bin full. Talk about your purveyors of darkness.

You are about to push that garlic through a garlic press that reminds Erin O'Brien of her favorite dildo, so practice some orchestration, if only for the sheer poetry of it. Feel that head of garlic up, babygirl. Make sure it's a good handful. You want it to be good and hard and bulbous with a certain heft that you can cup in your palm. *(shhhh, this is a secret... deriving pleasure from feeling up a head of garlic is the proper execution of life. Joy eludes those who search for it— 'tis true. The secret of life is in the palm of your hand. These are the things no one tells you.)*

Oh hell.

I've got to come clean right up front here.

When I make Hungarian lecho (pronounced letch-oh, sometimes spelled lecsó), not only am I a control freak on the hand-dice of the peppers and onion, I get all the ingredients prepared and lined up like some miserable Next Food Network Star wannabe, which is the modern refer-ence. If you're old school, you'll remember how the TV chefs would step onto the kitchen set and all these neat little bowls filled with chopped whatnot would be in front of them ready to go. The Cajun Cook (Justin Wilson) or the Galloping Gourmet (Graham Kerr) would make everything look oh-so-easy while we real Real Housewives knew that backstage, some poor lackey was slicing his fingers to shreds as he carved out interior pepper ribs and cried his eyes out over a pile of minced onions.

Welcome to the real world, sugartits.

Pry off two or three cloves of garlic from that funky head (although sometimes I use four because I am completely righteous) and crush those through the press that reminds Erin O'Brien of a speculum. Put the sticky lump into its very own dish. And yes, I use little dishes for the little ingredients and bigger dishes for the more voluminous ingredients. Poetry, remember?

Next up: one big ol' green bell pepper and one big ol' sweet red bell pepper. Here I go with the persnickety neatness-counts spiel: clean out the ribs proper and cut those peppers into and about three-eighths-inch pieces as best you can. Put all those tidy red and green squares in another bowl.

Chop one large (bigger than your fist) sweet onion (the regular yellow cheap will do fine as well) into pieces about the same size as the peppers and put that in another bowl.

You're going to need two or three hot peppers, I use a combination of Hungarian, jalapeño, or habanero, whatever looks good at the market.

If I told you about the ingredient bowls, I guess I'd better just let out a big sigh and tell you about the gloves. That would be the candy-ass latex gloves that no real Hungarian should ever use, but I use them when I don't want to get icky meat stuff under my fingernails and sometimes when I'm up to my elbows in hot peppers. Do I like to admit that I use latex gloves in the kitchen? Hell no, I don't, but here I am just the same.

Why?

Because you're going to clean those peppers properly by removing the seeds and ribs and then giving them a very fine dice (about an eighth of an inch) and if you get that invisible pepper hotness on your hands and touch your eyes or (ahem) some other sensitive part of your body (not that I have any personal experience with this), you could be in a world of hurt.

If you don't use gloves (no way did the old-timers like Graham Kerr and Justin Wilson use gloves), just washing won't get that evil pepper hotness off your paws (just ask an old-timer Hungarian), but rubbing them down with olive oil will. Get down with a rub-a-dub-dub-dub of olive oil, and then wash thoroughly. You might want to test your fingertips with your tongue before embarking on any (ahem, ahem) intimate personal maintenance. Repeat with the oil and washing until the heat-bite is gone (unless of course you're into that sort of thing [you're on your own]). Put the hot peppers into another bowl.

Here is another big sigh moment. How does one person who's been making Hungarian lecho her whole life tell another person about the sausage you should be using for said Hungarian lecho? Here in Cleveland, we've got Dohar Meats, which makes a double smoked extra spicy garlic sausage that kicks ass and produces the best lecho I've ever had, hands down.

I. Cannot. Do. Everything. For. You. People.

Oh sure, you could go to the regular grocery and buy a fourteen-ounce-it's-not-even-a-whole-pound-anymore package of that plastic wrapped crap that thinks it's smoked sausage but is really just a big hot dog with tons of sodium nitrate and loads of gross unidentifiable chewies (cartilage pieces and bits of tubes, etc.) that defy mastication, but please don't. Go find a decent Eastern European butcher who makes his own sausages and smoked and cured meats. Tell him you're making lecho. He may or may not know what you're talking about. Tell him it's a Hungarian hot pepper relish served with smoked sausage. Get his recommendation. Ask for a sample. You're looking for something that's meaty and smoky. If it's spicy and garlicky to boot, that's all the better. Buy about a pound, maybe a little more.

Hold on one second. Since we're here. Go on and check if that butcher makes his own smokies. Pick up a few links of those if he does. That doesn't have anything to do with the lecho, but homemade smokies are one of the reasons it's great to be a human, a bonus of sorts for having to endure poison ivy and embarrassing odors. Plus, your menfolk love these things.

Slice your sausage into quarter-inch thick discs (or just a tad bigger) and put them in another bowl.

Melt a tablespoon or so of butter in a pan (I use a 3" deep 12" skillet with a good lid [as in the proper fitting lid that goes with the skillet and not a lid that belongs to another pan that you're using because you can't find the proper lid in the impossible Drawer of Lids that is a construct straight from the depths of hell]) with about three tablespoons of olive oil and heat 'r up. (Will I tell anyone if you plop a spoonful of bacon fat in there? Hell no, I won't tell anyone if you plop a spoonful of bacon in there.) Throw in the onion and sauté that for about two minutes on medium. Add the red and green sweet peppers and sauté for another two minutes. (Yes, I use the timer. No, I don't like to admit it. You can file that in the same category as the latex gloves and the pre-organized bowls of ingredients.)

Turn the heat down to medium low and add the hot peppers and garlic, two tablespoons of water, a tablespoon of Worcestershire, a tablespoon of Tabasco (yes, a whole tablespoon—or more), a half-cup of ketchup, and salt and crushed red pepper to taste. (When I say taste, it should be HOT. This is lecho and it's supposed to be kick-ass hot, not just "spicy" hot. It should be hot enough to separate the men from the boys or the quirky half-breed Irish Hungarian broads from the Stepford wives.) Don't forget the paprika—a teaspoon or so, more if you're dealing with your old-timers.

Stir everything up and add the sausage.

Give it another stir and cover that mother up. Adjust the heat until you get a nice low simmer and let it ride for 15 or 20 minutes. No, you don't need to stir it (but it's okay if you do). No, you won't blow the whole thing if take a peek because you're an impatient dumbass (which I [being completely perfect] have never, ever, ever done). Just make sure you get 15 minutes of solid simmering, because that's what it takes to make lecho magic happen. The mystery going on inside that pan is not for comprehension by mere mortals, so don't try and figure it out. But all those ingredients that looked raw are turning into a rich hot spicy relish that is fit for the gods as well as a middle class suburban housewife. Don't believe me? Go on and lift the lid and behold your Hungarian lecho.

Let out a big sigh of your own.

Add more hot sauce or crushed red pepper if it's not

hot enough, another shake of salt or paprika if it needs it. Whatever you do, take this advice: make this stuff a day before you're going to serve it. Because if you think it's kick-ass now, it's going to be even kick-assier after 24 hours on account of the flavors "marrying." (See? I can use important chef terms with the best of them.)

Serve the lecho piping hot with crackers or small bread rounds as a cocktail snack (and I'm using the word "cocktail" reluctantly—lecho is classic Hungarian drinking food: the more you eat, the more you can drink). That's my favorite way to eat lecho, but people also eat it over rice or noodles or dumplings as a main course. I've been known to spoon it over leftover mashed potatoes for lunch or even over scrambled eggs for breakfast.

I love lecho.

That said, I have a sad cultural addendum to this recipe. Back in the 70s when my mom would make lecho and take it to a party, every last bit would be scraped from the dish. Now when I whip up a batch to take to the potluck, there are almost always leftovers. Oh sure, your old-timer holdout guys belly up, but the general American palate has pretty much turned candy ass.

Who cares?

I will be making hot Hungarian lecho until the day I die.

A KitchenAid is Forever

In 1993, My Gram Soos's neighbor, the Widow Clake, died at age 97. The mourning Clakes converged on the dearly departed's apartment and did what families do at such junctures: painfully sorted through the miscellany left behind in their loved one's wake. One of the items no one wanted was an ancient K4-B KitchenAid mixer. Gram watched on from her peephole as it was unceremoniously relegated to the dumpster.

When nary a Clake was in sight, she tiptoed from her apartment and heaved the K4-B out of the trash.

"Erin will know what to do with this," she mused. It weighed 23 pounds.

Not only did Gram pull out the mixer, she salvaged two mixing bowls, the dough hook, beater and whipper attachments, as well as the instruction and recipe booklet. In it, befreckled children worthy of Mayberry grin over plates of fruit drop cookies and housewives of the 1940's swoon over the KitchenAid as if it was Vic Damone in the buff. "Meet your KitchenAid!" it espouses.

We got the K4-B home, muscled it onto the counter, plugged it in and powered her up. Screeches and squeals erupted, but the beater shaft rotated perfectly.

"I'll oil it," said my husband.

If the Vita-Mix is a caped superhero and the garlic press is a schizophrenic sex fiend in disguise, then the K4-B is a stoic soldier on an endless march. Despite it's advanced age (it was manufactured in Troy, Ohio by Hobart in the late 1940s), my KitchenAid makes soft peaks out of egg whites, takes Dream Whip to cloud nine and elevates the mashed potato to a fluffy spud. So move over Cinderella and make room for the KitchenAid. After all, it went from a trash heap to living happily ever after in Erinland.

A few years after this divine arrangement began, my husband's Aunt Florence went to join her dearly departed husband at age 86. Just like the Clake clan, we Nowjacks convened at Aunt Florence's place and started sorting through her utensil drawers and linen closet. My brother-in-law and I were sent to see about the basement. Somewhere between the Sunday clothes enveloped in plastic and Uncle Louie's meticulously labeled tool organizer, we unearthed a K4-B, which looked exactly like mine and was in excellent condition. Unlike the Clakes, we knew that this was a keeper.

"What's this?" said my brother-in-law, reaching for a cardboard box that was nestled next to the K4-B. It was marked "KitchenAide FC meat grinding attachment", and that is exactly what was in it.

Everyone agreed that my brother-in-law, who is king of the kitchen in his house and has fed our collective tribe any number of sloppy joes, pork roasts and vegetable trays, should keep Aunt Florence's K4-B.

"You keep this," he said of the meat grinding attachment. "I'll never use it."

"You sure?" I asked, already grabbing the box.

"Yeah, yeah," he insisted, "and if I ever need it, I know where to find it."

I brought the dull aluminum appendage home and stashed it on a shelf in the utility room. For five years it remained, marking the passage of time with an ever-thickening layer of dust—until one lofty Sunday morning.

"Would you look at this," I said to my husband as we perused the paper. "Sirloin is on sale for $2.99 a pound. I paid $3.99 that for ground round last week!"

And with that, a private *ting* chimed in my head.

"And?" said my husband. I didn't answer. I was already en route to the utility room. In no time, I had the K4-B in the center of the kitchen counter, with the FC meat grinder secured in the attachment socket. Off to the grocery I went.

Back home, I considered the plastic-wrapped slab of meat. I would have to cut it into pieces that would fit into the grinder's feeding tube. So be it. I furiously went to work and soon I had a bowl full of glistening red cubes.

I turned on the K4-B's speed control lever to 1 (it goes to 10). The grinder began rotating politely. I dropped in one cube of meat after another, pushing them down with the handle of a spatula. After the third or forth deposit, a slurping squish sound indicated that the meat was finally being ground. I upped the speed control to 3 and stepped up my feed-rate. The noises ratcheted up as well, including wet pops and sucking sounds. The whole affair would have done well as a would-be voice over for an adult film.

After what seemed like an eternity, long pink worms of beef began extruding from the grinder's production holes. The resulting pile in the collection bowl looked every bit as good as the hundreds of packages I've pulled from butcher cases over the years, maybe even better.

"Aha!" I said victoriously to no one, shoving in another cube.

Then I felt something, a tiny sensation on my face, an itty-bitty painless prick. Then another. And another and another. My brow twisted in confusion as my husband walked in. He paused, shifted his eyes from me to the bowl of raw meat to the dripping grinder. He cleared his throat and walked back out without a word. I turned off the machine and fingered my cheek, where I found dots of wetness. I drew back my hand for further inspection

Blood.

Tiny splashes of blood. They were everywhere, on me, the counter, the kitchen floor. It was some unholy combination of Steven King's *Carrie* and A Housewife's ode to Jeffrey Dahmer.

No matter how I might jest about processing my husband through the Vita-Mix, standing in my kitchen covered in blood droplets while grinding raw meat was patently unacceptable. I wiped my face, sponged the various surfaces.

Then I got a dishtowel and tented it over the K4-B, leaving only the feed tube exposed. (An effective method unless the operator [not me–never, ever me] is careless about the application of said dishtowel to said mixer during, say, the whipping of chocolate mousse, and a corner of said towel gets tangled in the beater mechanism during operation, which produces an avant-garde moving interactive sculpture of sorts that one might title "Study in Chocolate Cotton Tornado"). With the splatter effectively stymied, I cranked up the speed switch and dropped in another cube of meat.

After all the cubes were process, I lifted the bloodied cloth and revealed a housewife's dream: a towering pile of ground meat and endless possibilities.

One Pound, One Pan, One Happy Family

I was running through the grocery at 100 MPH, which I always do, and which always strikes me as silly since my meager professional requirements have no scripted hours. Yet there I was, rushing like an idiot against some unseen stopwatch that constantly screams at me: *you're not carpe-ing enough of the goddamn diem!* My shopping list was crumpled between my sweaty hand and the handle of my cart. Every item was scratched off save DINNER?!!, which had been written in desperation and with no small about of hope that a in-store revelation would solve the obvious dilemma. These people want to eat Every Single Day. It's downright irritating.

"What's for dinner?" my daughter asks.

What's for dinner? What'sfordinner? What'sfordinne rdinnerdinnerdinner?

HELL IF I KNOW!

I stopped suddenly, my breath slightly exaggerated from my frenzied shopping. Perhaps by divine guid-ance, I found myself in the "boxed dinners" aisle of the grocery store before some two-dozen different varieties of Hamburger Helper.

Hamburger Helper.

Ham.

Bur.

Ger.

Hel.

Per.

It was as if I'd never acknowledged its existence before that moment. Never before had I purchased or eaten Hamburger Helper, although someone could have slipped me a scoop of it at a potluck. Who knows? I blinked at the fully stocked shelves, transfixed and giddy. At once, the glorious light spilled upon me: *I'm making Hamburger Helper for dinner!*

I was going to bask in the American housewife's dream of a smiling bright-faced family with bowls of steaming goodness in front of them after just 15 minutes of practically effortless mixing and simmering. Why, it would be just like the back of the box says: "One pound. One pan. One happy family."

But which flavor to select? Philly Cheese steak or Cheesy Baked Potato or Tomato Basil Penne? We gots us some delicious Cheesy Hashbrowns and Potato Stroganoff and Cheesy Jambalaya. There was Cheddar Cheese Melt and Chili Cheese and Chili Macaroni and and and... Cheesy weezy sneezy! My head spun with the possibilities.

If a regular person is going to make Hamburger Helper, I thought, a regular person ought to make regular Hamburger Helper. Cheeseburger Macaroni struck me as regular. I plucked a box from the shelf with a self-satisfied nod and floated off to the check out aisle.

At home, the package instructed me to brown a pound of ground beef and drain (can do!); add 2 cups milk and 1 1/4 cups HOT water (yes sir!); and stir in the Sauce Mix and uncooked Pasta (I'm on it!). Then I was to bring that baby to a boil, reduce the heat, cover it all and settle in while it simmered for "about 14 minutes."

Mother fucker, I thought, *why didn't I jump on this beautiful bandwagon sooner?*

But as I began stepping through the process, I found it to be synthetic and slightly forced in a masturbating-with-your-left-hand sort of way. The macaroni looked like plastic, with noodles that were shorter and fatter than the good Lord intended. The "Sauce Mix" was powdered orange stuff. And dumping milk onto ground beef? I gulped down my distaste and popped a Stroh's as a buffer of sorts during the 14-minute simmering period.

The timer went off. I uncovered my piping-hot home-made meal. "Doesn't look so bad," I said.

"What are those?" asked my kid, wrinkling her nose and pointing at one of several gooey orange blobs.

"Presumably chunks of the powdered cheese sauce that I failed to sufficiently stir in," I said.

"What is 'sufficiently?'" she asked.

But I was captivated by the skillet before me. "It means ... something... " I replied vacantly.

"What if it's no good?" she said.

"Then we give it to your father."

"All of it?"

"Yes," I said.

"And he'll eat it?" she asked.

"Yes."

"Poor Dad."

"Dinner!" I chirped gleefully as I loaded up three dishes and sashayed over to the table.

We took our places. My husband shoveled in a forkful and chewed indifferently. My kid heaved a big sigh and looked down at her plate. I smiled pure cheer around the table and took a tentative mouthful. We chewed, eyes darting from our respective servings of Hamburger Helper to each other to miscellaneous points around the room. I swallowed hard.

If you took any cheeseburger product from beneath the Golden Arches, dehydrated it, stored the resulting powder inside a cardboard box for several months and then recon-stituted it and ate it, I think you would have an epicurean experience preferable to that of the realized Hamburger

Helper. It didn't even taste like food, but instead some alien interpretation of human foodstuff, what Gort might concoct in his steely spaceship lab in order to feed all of humankind.

I cleared my throat and took another mouthful to give my first impression some additional experience. I bit down only to release an explosion of MSG and modified cornstarch against the roof of my mouth. Undoubtedly one of the gooey "Cheese Sauce" bombs had just unleashed its villainous secrets. I swallowed it down along with my grimace. I didn't want my daughter to catch on.

Any other forward-thinking practitioner of Home Economics would have looked at her loving family with a conciliatory smile and said, "Oh all right, I'll steam some fresh broccoli and salmon." Not me.

"Eat it," I commanded.

I doused my dish with hot sauce, which is the course of action to take when confronted with any inedible foodstuff. Add enough Frank's Red Hot (utility grade) or Tabasco (old school) or Habanera sauce (the advanced class) and you can't taste anything. I used Frank's for the Helper as it has additional salt and a bit of vinegar and the Helper needed all the help it could get. My husband and kid turned to their plates with dread.

My husband ate his stoically. "Might as well be done with it," he said gravely as he walked to the table with heaping helping number two. Is there any question why this man gets whatever he wants in the bedroom?

"You were right, Mom," said my kid, watching him with awe. "He is going to eat it all." She used her fork to plow yet another cheese sauce powder blob over to the segregated collection of same on her plate. "Do NOT eat those," she warned then slowly forked one of the mutant macaronis.

"You're too late," I said.

"Do I have to eat it all?" she asked.

"It's just like a Micky-D cheeseburger mixed up with Kraft Macaroni and Cheese," I said, naming two of my daughter's favorites.

"Sure, Mom," she said, drawing out the -om in that low skeptical tone she saves for occasions when even I don't believe what I'm saying.

"Just be thankful," I said, setting down my fork and leveling my eyes to hers, "that it's not slumgullion."

At that moment, I had no idea how or why that word came to me, I hadn't uttered it in years, much less eaten the dish it represented. But for some reason, slumgullion had re-entered my life. There it was, stubborn and irrefutable: slumgullion.

Now it had to be gotten through like all the rest of it.

###

The slumgullion experience of my youth always started off with a pound of raw hamburger on the kitchen counter. My father would pluck a chunk from it as my mother admonished him.

"But that's for the slumgullion!" she'd say.

Undeterred, he would sprinkle the meat with salt and pop it into his mouth en route to his downstairs machine shop.

Then Mom would slumgullify the wormy red mass by browning it, draining off the fat and adding terrifying ingredients. In went Monday's spaghetti, the oily onion and green pepper dregs from Tuesday's pepper steak, and the remainder of Wednesday's succotash (which included both lima beans and—god help us—hominy). Throughout the process, my brother and I exchanged looks of unified dread that culminated in silent mastication at the dinner table.

Slumgullion.

The name alone is hard to swallow. It's like a slug in a guillotine in a slum. It's an awful word the way crotch is an awful word. Who says, "Oh baby, I want to dive into your crotch"? No one says that. It's gross. "So baby, howzabout some slumgullion?" isn't much better.

Completely unreliable online historians trace slumgullion back to a) the watery refuse resulting from whale blubber processing, b) a dish made from slaughterhouse cast-offs in the slums of England in the late 1800s, or c) a thin stew California miners made from leftovers during the Gold Rush. Who cares which checkered past is accurate? Any one of them beats that candy-ass three-fingered Hamburger Helper glove.

Every slumgullion recipe is different. People add cheese, tomato sauce, bacon, frozen peas, macaroni—name your poison. I've heard of people using (help) canned corned beef. Others use condensed soup to tie it all together. (Admittedly, I practically deify a can of Campbell's cream of mushroom. If you can't turn one of those into dinner in 20 minutes, you're no housewife in my book. But if you transform a can of Campbell's cream of whatever into a platter of Company Chicken Supreme in a wink, you're in).

So what would Eringullion look like? Surely I could do better than that Betty Crocker broad and her boxed Cheeseburger Macaroni. Recreating mom's recipe was no fun. I needed to update and modernize the slumgullion concept while keeping it firmly entrenched in its ground-beef-and-ingredients-on-hand birthright. Even if I didn't have any leftovers, the slumgullion should feel leftovery: refrigerator round-up in a pan.

I chose onion, green pepper, a can of creamed corn,

one of RoTel's original tomato concoctions, three old potatoes, (each with a host of gnarly eyes), some Worchester sauce, and a mysterious seasoning called "Rich Brown" that costs 50 cents for a box of eight packets at the discount grocery. This darling concoction of MSG, maltodextrin, onion powder, caramel color, spices, disodium guanylate and disodium inosinate was, according to the package, "a delicious broth and a seasoning that brings out the best in food flavors." *I am all over that*, I thought.

Unlike the Hamburger Helper experience, as soon as I started making the slumgullion, familiarity washed over me. *You're home*, assured a soft voice inside my head as I doused the diced onion with Mazola. Why, this was innate. Even the creamed corn that I had included as a mandatory "yuck" ingredient formed a beautiful golden pool when I poured it atop the beef. The slumgullion terrors of my childhood were all but gone, a harmless wisp. By the time I added the canned tomatoes and chiles, I was grinning from ear to ear and singing "Slum-gull-yon. Slum-slum-slum-gull-yon" to the tune of "Girl from Ipanema." I sprinkled a packet of Rich Brown over it all and sighed contentedly.

Ten minutes before dinner, I moved through the house like an old-fashioned hotel page. "Slumgullion minus ten," I lilted. "That's slumgullion minus ten."

If I thought the Hamburger Helper instilled fear in my kid, the slumgullion was sheer terror on a plate. She stared at it wordlessly.

I transformed into my mother. "Eat your slumgullion," I said. She wrinkled her nose and took a bite, swallowing over a gag.

"Oh, come on," I said, "it's delicious!"

"Not bad," said my dearly beloved before taking a sip of Matthew Fox cabernet ($3.29/bottle at the discount grocery). "It's nothing special, but it's not bad."

I let his shocking assessment settle for a moment while blinking at him in disbelief.

"Nothing special?" I said indignantly as I rose to get another helping. "What do you mean 'nothing special'?" I turned from the stove to see my daughter quickly set down her plate, from which she'd dumped three-quarters of her slumgullion onto my husband's dish. "It beats the hell of that miserable Hamburger Helper!" I said.

Silence.

"Well?" I said, "doesn't it?" My eyes shifted between my husband and daughter. "Beat the Hamburger Helper?"

My kid cowered before my arched eyebrows. "Um ... " she peeped. I glared in disapproval then turned to my splendid king with pursed lips.

"The leftover Hamburger Helper was better the next day," he said in a conciliatory tone. "Maybe the slumgullion will be better tomorrow."

I let "better tomorrow" float in the air for a handful of

beats as my chest pumped short angry breaths and I glowered at him.

"Well. You. Miserable. Goat." I finally said, pronouncing each word in a low deliberate voice. Then I stood.

"Honey?" said the Goat. "I didn't mean anything." He paused, waiting. "Honey?"

"Nevermind," I said in a high thin voice, then sniffed and retrieved my shoes from the steps.

"What are you doing?" he said.

"Nothing."

"Mom?"

"Forget it." I tied my shoes with force and stood, set my jaw and squared my shoulders. As my family asked after me, I stepped out the front door and began walking the earth, never more alone.

Evil Forces vs. Home Economic Warriors

As is abundantly apparent in these pages, I spend an inordinate amount of time at the discount grocery. Up and down the cramped aisles therein, domestic warriors like myself battle the evil foes that constantly conspire against us.

We all watched on as the venerable half-gallon of ice cream shrunk to one and three-quarters quarts. Then it went to a quart and a half in one leap. Will the actual half-gallon ever return or must I forever settle on the generic brands that concede the full half gallon at the expense of ingredients (goodbye cane sugar, hello high fructose corn syrup)?

To hell with germs, I want to use that paper bathroom cup for at least two brushings. But the glue that adheres the side seam begins disintegrating as soon as it gets wet and the cup is reduced to a pulpy mess that is barely serviceable by the time I reach the denouement of my morning oral routine–the final rinse (performed with Swan Original Antiseptic Mouth Rinse, which is not only ADA accepted, but also includes active ingredients that the label encourages me to compare to that of a leading national brand [I have], which is three times the cost of the Swan brand thank you very much).

Then there is the impossible prospect of the last few ounces of laundry detergent, which are patently inaccessible due to the no-drip spout on the bottle (a point I grudgingly concede because I remember the days of the gooey jug of Tide when it looked like the Frankenstein version of an empty Chianti bottle caked with the wax tears of so many candles). So there I am every few weeks risking life and limb, jamming a flimsy paring knife against the thick orange plastic Tide jug where it bows threateningly and eventually pierces same. Then I am able to carve a triangular emergency escape hole through which the last drops of Tide will, as the product's name implies, flow unfettered.

Coupons, buy-one-get-one, Sunday circulars: I fight the good fight. I get the last drop, choose Suave over Pantene, and rinse and reuse long after the manufacturer recommends. You'll find me sniffing around the closeout and clearance aisles, from whence I buy the seconds, argue for another ten percent off and amass my mismatched household items such as towels and flatware and plates for pennies on the dollar.

Never was the acumen of my adversaries more apparent then on the day when I stood before the rows of Colgate-

Eventually alone, I glanced around sheepishly then put the delightfully perfumed Lavender and Chamomile SoftSoap back on the shelf (yes, I unscrewed the top in order to take a sniff and yes, I screwed it back on properly) and picked up a 99-cent bottle of Lucky SuperSoft Premium Liquid Hand Soap, which, as another clandestine sniff verified, was not nearly as fragrant to me as the Colgate-Palmolive offerings, but had a suction tube that went all the way to the bottom by god!

An innocence is lost; some disapproval is earned; and a mandate reigns in the sensual pleasure of smell. The point of all this scrimping is that, if I do it successfully and relentlessly, once in a while I can capitalize the L in luxury. Once in a while, I can afford to plop a lobster in my factory-second pot.

On Flying Lobsters

We had been married two years when my mother-in-law gave me the cleaver.

"My mother used to use one just like this to cut up the lobster for the lobster and rice," she told me. The knife was heavy, with a thick steel blade that measured about three by six inches.

"Whoa," I said with respect as I hefted it. Owning such a knife was clearly a right of passage. I had no idea what to do with it. My mother-in-law, however, had an ulterior motive.

About six months after she gave me the knife, Pat invited us out for dinner. Near the end of the evening, she lifted her purse onto the table with her painfully arthritic hands and pulled out a yellowed index card on which the following was hand-written:

Lobster and Rice

Cut up live lobster.
Remove sac from underneath head and black insides.

*Sauté with minced garlic, parsley and fresh mint in
Mazola oil for 15-20 minutes.*

*Add 2 heaping teaspoons tomato paste mixed with
water.*

Add rice with enough water to cook rice thoroughly.

"Remember the lobster and rice I was telling you about?" she said. "That's the recipe."

Okay, I thought, *Okay already. I get the hint.*

Standing before the lobster tank in the upscale grocery, my attention was drawn to the three lobsters in the back of the tank based largely on their separation from the other lobsters, which were in an unseemly stack near the front of the tank. These three—what were quickly becoming *my* three—were in their own arena. The two larger ones were alternately advancing and retreating with their banded claws raised up like angry fists. The third was spinning around drunkenly and bucking in that odd backwards manner of lobsters. I was always instructed to select lobsters based on their diametric opposition to the proceedings, so when the lady with the hair net and the big plastic lobster grabber asked me, "Which ones?" I said, "gimme those three mean ones in the back."

She muscled the first two into a cheerful carrying box that featured a colorful drawing of lobsters that were much happier than mine and the suggestion to *Enjoy!* She went in for number three.

"What you got here," said the lady as she battled it, "is essentially a one and a half pound cockroach with hella attitude." She gave up on the lobster grabber and rolled up her sleeve, then plunged her arm into the tank. "Christ that's cold!" The lobster scurried across the tank in an effort to join the pile of dullards, but she bested it, hoisted it out, and held it up victoriously. The lobster responded by stretching out its tail and mightily displaying its claws as if to say you *sonsabitches ain't won just yet.* The lady's smock was splotched with water.

"Gotcha a good one here," she said. She put it in its own carrier box.

I agreed, thanked her and apologized for her inconvenience, although I was not entirely sure she hadn't enjoyed the fray. After all, the lobsters served up real action. Where's the thrill of slapping tilapia filet atop a scale?

I have introduced many a lobster to a pot of boiling water and I can attest that when Irma S. Rombauer, Marion Rombauer Becker and Ethan Becker assert in *The All New All Purpose Joy of Cooking*, that, "it is unlikely, say most experts, that lobsters feel pain," the group of experts included in the associated interview were not lobsters. When you drop a lobster into a pot of boiling water, the miserable bastard thrashes like hell for a few seconds, which always feels longer than it is and makes me feel like a murderous louse until I get over it and take comfort in the fact that I am a human, it is a crustacean, and therefore, I win.

So I had some experience with live lobsters, which had theretofore included going from the grocery's cute little lobster box to pot, sometimes with an interlude in the kitchen sink where the out-of-water lobsters would lie, their antennae weirdly pointing around the kitchen as if trying to tune into a secret broadcast on an escape route. (If lobsters could depict such a scene on film, would they not, at such a juncture, include an ardent voice-over in the manner of a sweat-sheathed silver-screen hero lashed and writhing beneath a swinging pendulum? *Just … need … to find … a way … out … don't … lose … hope …* Alas, the lobsters in my sink have never achieved what our onscreen hero always seems to pull off at the last minute.)

My mother-in-law's favorite dish, however, required a more elaborate preparation. I retrieved the lobster and rice recipe card.

Cut up live lobster.

Okay, fine. Sounded simple enough. I plopped the first lobster on my cutting board and wielded the cleaver that started it all. I set my jaw and took a firm hold of the lobster with my other hand, heretofore oblivious of the little flippers (swimmerets) on the backside of the tail, which were flipping like mad.

The tightening of my grip coincided with the moment the sensory receptors on my fingertips acknowledged the wet, oily and frantic swimmerets, thereby sending a message to my brain: *you've got your hands around a one and a half pound cockroach!*

"WAAAHRGH!"

I jumped, sending the lobster sailing along a parabolic trajectory through the kitchen. It landed in front of the patio door with a wet splat/crack. I huffed a few breaths, looked to and fro in the silence and went to assess the damage. There I stood, looking down at a lobster splayed upon my linoleum floor.

"Shit."

I picked it up only to discover that its flight and subsequent landing had not diminished its defiance. It stretched out as strongly as it had when the grocery lady plucked it from the tank (assuming this was the same one who had engaged us in that performance; who can tell one lobster from another lobster?). I held it by the solid body, away from the gross-me-out swimmerets. I swallowed hard in determination, rinsed it off and set the lobster back upon the cutting board.

After raising the cleaver, losing my gall, setting it back down, grimacing, swearing, putting my hand on my hip and looking at various points around the kitchen for moral support, and repeating this sequence in varying order a few times, I eventually mustered enough courage to bring the cleaver crashing into the lobster's body.

I didn't do it quite courageously enough.

Instead of severing the lobster in half, the blade only went about three-quarters of the way through. The lobster thrashed and flipped, releasing a stinky black liquid that squirted out, then oozed over the cutting board and Formica countertop, down the cabinets and onto the floor.

By that time, I was more or less swearing unfettered, although the inky dousing evoked a few particularly fervent expletives. It also marked the lobster's demise. It weakened, but still offered lingering spasms as I severed the claws, tail and legs.

One down, two to go. At least I hadn't thrown up yet.

Since the first surgery had been hugely objectionable for me as well as the lobster, I figured it was time to solicit advice from my cookbooks. I needed a break anyway. I fanned through my books and perused the indices, eventually finding a photo of a lobster on its back with a man's hand holding the claws in a cross above the lobster's head. This procedure, I was informed, immobilized said lobster. Using a paring knife, I was to stab the lobster in the center of the thorax below the head and drive the knife downward through the body with a sawing motion.

Despite the fact that "thorax" reminded me of Dr.

Seuss's environmentally cautioning Lorax, I soldiered on even though stabbing and eviscerating the lobster wasn't all that much better than lopping it in half with a cleaver. Although, between the flipper swimmerets and screaming and flopping, maybe the cleaver wasn't all that great an idea after all. I wasn't accustomed to it and therefore didn't wield it with the advanced level of skill one should have when employing such a formidable tool. Hell, I was unfamiliar with the whole process, but stabbing a finger with a paring knife was better than lopping it off with a cleaver. Plus, I had a wicked little blade that seemed perfectly suited for the job.

Holding the lobster down by its claws did immobilize it; the tail stayed flat on the cutting board, although the swimmerets still did their dance. I had a few false starts, bringing the dagger-like knife to within a centimeter of the body and stopping short as the ghost of Seuss's darling little mustachioed Lorax floated behind me. Finally, I managed to stab straight through the body as tears squeezed from the corners of my eyes. The sound was short-lived, but terrible. And no, the lobster did not die immediately as the book promised (although there may have been a teeny-weeny bit of operator error involved). I had to saw down through the body in order to finish it off. Then I dismembered it, gagging and grimacing and swearing the whole time. And yes, those goddamn flippers and legs kept up with the spasms throughout—even when they were just parts in a bowl.

You never imagine yourself dismembering a lobster in your kitchen until you're actually dismembering a lobster in your kitchen.

I'm leaving out some of the lobster and expletive hurls, and the pauses spent huffing over the kitchen sink like an overblown horror movie starlet catching her breath just after she's stabbed the serial killer through the eyehole of his hockey mask with a pair of sewing sheers, but I eventually murdered and dismembered all three lobsters. Before me was a bowl upon which might have been printed, "lobster parts R US."

I had achieved the first directive on the recipe card and was ready to move on.

Remove sac from underneath head and black insides.

The kitchen floor, the counters, the Erin—everything was covered in lobster guts and splintered shell pieces and that inky liquid. The three eviscerated lobster torsos were grotesquely arranged on the cutting board. It seemed I'd already "removed" the "black insides." Now I was supposed to go digging around for a "sac?"

Fuck that!

I mean, how many guts could be left in there? I sighed

and snorted and grunted, not wanting to come to terms with the fact that this was obviously a pretty Spartan recipe and if it said to cut out the insides and sac, I probably had to cut out the insides and sac.

I picked up one of the bodies and used the knife to pry open the severed shell. It wasn't pretty. But the image of my mother- and father-in-law clutching their throats as they succumbed to some mysterious lobster gut poisoning wasn't so good either. I went in.

Removing the squishy slimy innards garnered the most ardent gagging of the entire event, but remove them I did. Satisfied that I'd completed the most taxing part of the proceedings, I mopped my sweaty brow, cracked open a beer and considered the remainder of the recipe.

Sauté with minced garlic, parsley and fresh mint in Mazola oil for 15-20 minutes.

Add 2 heaping teaspoons tomato paste mixed with water.

Add rice with enough water to cook rice thoroughly.

As a chunk of tail twitched in the bowl at my elbow, I was left with more uncertainty about how to proceed than direction. How much water? How long should the rice cook? What about the shells?

I knew what I had to do: go to the source. My mother-in-law was a first generation Greek American who grew up in New Bedford, Massachusetts: the whaling capitol, the land of Ishmael and *Moby Dick* and Melville for chrissake! They practically have wild lobsters roaming the streets over there. Pat would know how to wrangle a bowl of twitching crustacean parts. Wasn't she the one who gave me the recipe in the first place? I picked up the phone.

"What do I do with the bodies?" I asked.

"What bodies?" she said.

"The center lobster body part thingies?"

"Oh I don't know anything about that," she said with a tone that indicated the question itself was ridiculous.

"How much rice do I put in?"

"You will not believe how delicious that rice is after you cook it with the lobster."

"But how much?" I asked again. "Rice?"

"You put in the rice and you cook it."

"Pat," I finally said. "Have you ever made lobster and rice?"

"Why would I make lobster and rice? My mother made the lobster and rice. Call Stella."

Aunt Stella was my mother-in-law's sister. She would know what to do, after all she was ten years older than Pat and still lived in New Bedford.

"What about all the cracked shells?" I asked Aunt Stella. "Do I just leave the shells like this?"

"It's a lobster in a shell," she said. "Don't you have the recipe?"

"Yeah, I have the recipe," I said. "I have YiaYia's recipe right here in front of me. It doesn't say anything about the shells."

"Lobsters have shells."

"Do you remember how she made the rice?"

"Sure, she cooked the rice," she said. "There was the lobster and there was the rice."

"Thanks Aunt Stella."

Sometimes you just have to handle it. I picked up the recipe card and sighed.

Fresh mint? What? Now I had to be some goddamn Martha-Stewart wannabe with a container herb garden on my windowsill? I didn't have any fresh mint. I didn't have any Mazola oil. I upended the olive oil over my biggest skillet and let it go glug glug glug a few times. I added a few shakes of dry parsley and some basil. Garlic? Four cloves sounded good. I crushed them through my (**sigh**) garlic press, added a whole can of tomato paste, mixed in some water and heated it all up. I dumped the lobster pieces into the pan, including the bodies. I awkwardly moved the whole mess around until the shells turned red. Then I dumped three cups of rice and six cups of water in there. I covered it and let it simmer until the water was absorbed by the rice.

When I removed the lid, I had lobster and I had rice (I figured the bodies had imparted all the flavor they were worth and took them out). I didn't know if I'd done good or bad, right or wrong, but the mission was accomplished.

Over the course of my married life, I've made lobster and rice five or six times. The butchering of the live lobsters has never gotten any easier. Each of my endeavors to cut up a live lobster was characterized by screaming, swearing, gagging and lobster hurling. I suppose it was worth it. My mother-in-law delighted in the fact that I would make her lobster and rice and if I had in fact botched it, she never let on. Every time I made the dish, save for the last time, my mother-in-law raved like it was fit for royalty.

The last time I made lobster and rice, it was a beautiful October day. We had recently acquired a picnic table and so I decided to chop the lobsters apart outside in order to cut down on the clean-up.

Other than the dazzling backdrop of gold, red and green leaves against a blue, blue sky, the scene was identical to what had transpired in my kitchen during previous lobster eviscerations. I even hurled a particularly ardent lobster across the yard and had to retrieve it from the bushes. My swearing was worthy of any men's locker room and loud enough to be enjoyed by the entire neighborhood.

I was making more lobster and rice than usual and

was between lobsters four and five when I heard the front doorbell through the screened patio door. I set down the lobster and the knife, wiped my hands across my filthy lobster-gut stained apron and went to answer it.

It was my neighbor Jane. She was holding a covered blue speckled roaster with two potholders.

"Roasted you a chicken," she said.

I swallowed hard. "Aw Jane," I said, hands on hips. "You can't imagine how much I appreciate that. I've been cooking all day—"

"—and you don't have a thing to eat," she said, finishing the sentence exactly as I had intended to. "I know."

Jane set the roaster down on the stove and hurried off to kids and errands and the miscellany of life. I returned to the lobsters.

That night, we ate Jane's chicken. It might have been the best chicken I'd ever had. The lobster and rice, along with all the other food I'd been preparing all day, sat in the refrigerator. There it would stay until I pulled it out the next day to take to my mother-in-law's wake.

Sweet Nothings for Ron Popiel
and the Secret of Hungarian Cucumbers

Let me whisper in your ear, baby.

You cannot know how I long to *set it and forget it*. And you are so right that I am not going to pay four hundred, or three hundred or even two hundred dollars. Yes, I want to unlock the health secrets of dehydrated banana chips, apples and apricots. I want to wait while you tell me that there is, in fact, more. Go ahead and chop all my onions, but I can't promise I won't shed a single tear. Show me the greatest kitchen appliance ever in the shape of a Chop-O-Matic and, baby, I'll gaze up at you with dewy eyes, shallow breath and fluttering heart.

Hundreds of potatoes transformed into French fries in minutes, beef jerky for three dollars a pound, and the banishment of slimy egg whites. You construct for me a world of perfection so sublime, I doth weep at your feet.

And what of the biggest fishing invention since the hook, the GLH-9 hair in a can and—be still my heart—Hey Good Lookin' I'll be back to pick you up later Mr. Microphone?

Dollar for dollar and homemade pasta and God Bless the Smokeless ashtray.

I so love you, baby.

###

Upon my countertop sits a Cuisinart Pro Custom 11 food processor. It came standard with a metal chopping blade, a dough blade, two slicing discs (2mm and 4mm) and a medium shredding disc. Over the years, I've added the DLC-834TX fine shredding disc and the CLC-846 6mm thick slicing disc to that collection.

Perhaps surprisingly, I am not on the verge of an orgiastic description of the joys of owning such a competent household appliance. No, Erin O'Brien is not about to gas on endlessly about the perfect uniformity of sliced carrot discs courtesy of the Cuisinart, the stalwart safety locks that keep the dangerous steel blade far from vulnerable human hand, and the suitable-for-a-Springbok-puzzle graphic provided by a feed tube properly loaded with upright celery sticks. After all, the modern food processor revolutionized kitchens from coast to coast and the Cuisinart is one of the best household models on the market, right?

Perhaps, but I hate it nonetheless.

The Pro Custom 11 fills me with shame. You use it, it works, that's it. Like a vapid automatic transmission on a Dodge Caravan, this piece of equipment has none of the inspirational user interface that the five-gear stick shift in my Mini Cooper provides. The Cuisinart sits smugly next to the oven, resolute with arrogance. *Don't you worry your pretty little head, Erin-O,* it whispers in a placating purr. *Mr. Cuisinart will do everything for you. Mr. Cuisinart slices. Mr. Cuisinart dices. Mr. Cuisinart juliennes.*

Mr. Cuisinart can kiss my ass.

No, the Pro Custom 11 wasn't a gift. Yes, I bought it myself. It represents the zenith of my failures, evidence that I have succumbed to the sanitized domestic experience I detest. It leaves no margin for error. Employing it is a zero risk experience. Load the feed tube with onions, engage your index finger and the patented Lexan bowl immediately fills with perfection. Even the two non-negotiable buttons "on" and "off-pulse" disgust me. Does the Cuisinart do the job? Sure, just like my spidery fingers produce a predictable and paltry orgasm. But to achieve a splendorous climax complete with grimacing and uncontrolled vocalization, that requires a more interactive approach with, say, seven and one-quarter silicone inches of the "Goliath" courtesy of your favorite online marital aid emporium and an unwitting UPS man, or better yet, an equal amount of the "Husband," courtesy of your sacred wedding vows.

Woe to he who cries, "Begone!" to the days of manual processing, whence the brick of Asiago thrummed against the grater, and the butcher knife hit home upon a solid cutting board with a satisfying whack. I remember with fondness the metallic taste of blood on my tongue as I slurped and sucked on a nicked knuckle or sliced fingertip.

Floating in the interim between days of yore and days of Cuisinart is perhaps the device over which I wax most nostalgic.

Thwack, thwack, thwack, went Ron Popeil's Deluxe Ronco Dial-O-Matic Food Cutter as I slid the convenient guide bar back and forth over the plastic carriage. At the tender age of nine, I was guiding green peppers to the land of perfect slice with nary a power cord in sight. Under my mother's approving gaze, I performed miracles with food, just like the box said.

Eventually the day came when Mom hauled out the cucumbers as well as the 50 percent Hungarian that bubbled inside of her. She dialed down the Ronco to a #2 thickness and set me on my way to becoming a master chef in minutes with Ron Popeil's fabulous device.

"It's time you learned how to make the cucumbers," she said to me.

###

There is a tiny rumble, a barely audible crackling in the East. It is the sound of the rummaging of kitchen drawers, from whence meat tenderizing mallets and wooden rolling pins are being drawn. The hands shuffling through the spatulas and pastry whisks and potato peelers belong to the fairer sex. They are old and pinched, their faces swaddled by scarves, their chins bristling with sparse black whiskers. They are young and comely, their smoky eyes lined in kohl, their lips lush and red, their full skirts gathered into cinching laces at the waist. They come from the banks of the Danube.

They are gathering in numbers, arming themselves with simple weapons. Soon they will come pouring from their tiny cottages with thatched roofs in the low mountains and from terraced townhouses that line the narrow streets of Budapest. They are convening in the tiny villages and big cities, forming an ever-growing sea of ample flesh that is bursting forth with indignant voices rising.

The object of their ire 'tis I, for I doth threaten to reveal their most precious secret!

Why? Because I just can't stand it. The very sight of you standing there with your pathetic Tupperware full up with ambrosia salad, potato salad, Cobb salad, Waldorf salad, or (good Christ) coleslaw racks me with disgust.

Is that really the best you can do? Why don't you just sign up for lifetime subscriptions to *Family Circle*, *Woman's World*, and *Redbook*, pack up the minivan and move the whole operation to Stepford? If you're dishing out that predictable slop, you're practically a robot already. To hell with the three-bean salad once and for all.

Let's go.

Get a few cucumbers, say three good-sized ones; we're talking about a pound each. (Heads-up: It takes two days to make this salad and plenty of hands-on labor. Now you know, so quit your bellyaching before it even starts.) Peel those cukes fine and hold one up for a good eyeful. Notice how the firm flesh glistens with its own juiciness. Look at the beautiful shape of the thing!

DO NOT cut that natural sculpture or scrape the seeds out or buy one of those genetic "seedless gourmet" monstrosities. You're talking nature's own regular slicing/ table cucumber.

We interrupt this recipe to bring you the following public service announcement:

Any consenting adult is duly encouraged to use any vegetable matter as a marital aid. Please carefully consider the following guidelines for a safe, convenient and enjoyable experience. Choose firm, high quality organically grown products. Wash vegetable matter first. Carving/ peeling vegetable matter into realistic shapes can make the experience whimsical and more satisfying. Any person who has used the vegetable matter as a marital aid is welcome to consume the vegetable matter after a thorough washing (of vegetable matter). DO NOT, however, serve the vegetable matter in question to parties who are unaware of the vegetable matter's previous employ, no matter how thoroughly they have been washed. Said practice is considered uncool.

We now continue with your regularly scheduled recipe, already in progress. Thank you.

Now you've got some options. You need to slice those cukes into discs about ¼" thick. It has to be real fine like artwork, and you'll need to choose your tool. As a kid, I sliced a mountain of cucumbers while at the helm of Ron Popeil's Dial-O-Matic vegetable slicer. When I took flight from the nest and first settled into holy matrimony, I didn't have a Dial-O-Matic, so I sliced the cukes by hand with varying degrees of success. Although I'm not proud to admit it, I eventually purchased my Cuisinart Pro Custom 11 on account of this Hungarian cucumber salad. And that miserable metrosexual of a household appliance does the job perfectly every single time. This saddens me.

With welling eyes, I feed the cukes down into that

voracious plastic tube and place my palm against the pusher assembly. Then I engage the 4mm slicing disc. Brrrrt goes the Pro Custom 11 and out come the cukes. In no time, they're all processed. I inhale a great lungful of air and remove the cover. The patented Lexan bowl is full-up with identical light green discs of gentle cucumber flesh surrounding delicate innards of seed and translucent pulp. I pick one up, place it upon my tongue and crush it slowly with my teeth before swallowing in defeat. I tell myself this does not make me less of a woman than the whiskered ladies of my Hungarian ancestry, but we all know that is a pathetic self-soothing lie.

Oh well.

You're about to use more salt in the next 15 minutes than you've used in the past 15 months.

You go on the Internet? You read some broad talking about her Hungarian cucumber salad? With her teaspoon of salt and her "let it sit for 45 minutes?" You listen to that and you know what you're going to end up with? A pile of dogshit, that's what. You just let ol' Erin tell you what it is.

Put a layer of those slices down at the bottom of a big mixing bowl. Salt the daylights out of that. I'm talking salt salt salt—your hand moving up and down like you're giving some maniacal upside-down air-guitar hand job. Another layer, more salt. Keep going until all the cucumber slices are gone and you've used enough salt to make your cardiologist start thinking about a color for his new Audi Roadster.

Cover that mother and put it in the fridge overnight. And don't be poking around in there. No stirring or draining or anything. Just leave it alone.

Take it out the next day and dump those babies in a salad spinner or colander. Pour off all that salty brine. Immerse the strainer in another bowl of fresh water and swish the cukes around. Lift the cukes out, get new water. Keep rinsing those cukes. Taste them. Too salty? Keep rinsing until the salt level is fly, then shake or spin off as much excess water as you can.

This ain't pretty, but it's the most important step, so get on it. You skip this and you might as well hang up your apron and schlep off to the Pizza Hut salad bar.

Get a dry bowl. Line it with a couple of paper towels. Take a handful of your cukes and squeeze the living daylights out of them. Get all the water out that you can. You have to do this with your hands. Don't think you're going to improvise with your potato ricer or your nancy French press coffee maker. This is one thing that miserable Cuisinart or any other device can't do. You need a regular human set of hands. Squeeze and shake and squeeze again.

Come on you bad kitty! Squeeze all that water out of

there!

When you've squeezed with all you've got and you open up your hand, the battered little wad of green is going to look sort of small and boogery. Don't fret, that's righteous. Plop it into the paper-towel lined bowl and get making with handful number two.

After about the third or fourth handful, you'll be praying for death. See if you can get your sig oth to come on over and help you squash all those effing cukes. Try saying this, "Hey sugar baby? Whyontcha come on and gimme a hand with these cukies?" real sweet-like.

Now the two of you are next to each other at the sink, squishing those slippery wet cucumbers between your fingers. You don't have to say a word. I know. Go on upstairs and take care of that proper. Because if you do, you just might be able to pull off this trick: in the fuzzy afterglow, burrow into the blankets and pillows all naked and full of purrs and—if your Karma is in good shape and the stars are in order and the ether immediately surrounding you is sparkling with good *chi*—your sig oth will look at you with big puppy eyes and see how you're all curled up and comfy and say, "You have a little nap here baby and I'll finish up squishing those old cucumbers." And then you doze and dream for a handful of luscious minutes while your sugarbaby does the cuke squeeze for you out of sublime love and sexual human contentment.

Wash your hands after you've been diddling around in bed like that for chrissake.

Give the cukes an extra squeeze and take out the paper towels. Mix in about a half cup of sour cream (whole fat, not that lame fat-free or reduced whatever) and about a quarter cup white vinegar. Don't get cutesy. No balsamic. No red wine. No malt schmalt. Just use the regular cheap Heinz that you buy at the discount grocery in the big plastic jug. Generic's fine too.

Stir it up proper. Now taste it. Add more sour cream to make it creamier. More vinegar to give it more tart, but careful not to put too much. Too much sour cream is no big deal, but put too much of that vinegar in there and you're done. Add paprika, salt and pepper to taste.

This is usually when you look into the bowl with bewilderment. Yes, you forgot something.

Oh yeah. The onion.

You should have added it before you did the vinegar and sour cream, but don't worry, it'll be fine. You need a good big one, about the size of your fist. Again, this is your regular cheap yellow. No heirloom, Vidalia or Spanish Red. Stop fooling around. Do it regular. Peel it and cut it in half from the top to the bottom hairy end. Good. Now slice that into thin, thin slices across the natural grain–so you end up with skinny half-circles when it comes apart. Stop crying like a nancy girl. It's not that hot. You want to use the Pro

Custom 11, go ahead. I've given that thing enough airtime as it is, so you're on your own there. Put all that sliced onion in those cukes.

Mix it so it gets a little foamy. Cover it and let it sit in the fridge for at least four hours or better yet, overnight.

Now take those cukes to your sister-in-law's house for the Fourth of July barbecue. Set it out next to the lame-o macaroni salad. Don't say one word, just put a slotted spoon in there and let that mother ride. Watch old Jimbo take a bite and say, "Holy Christ that's a cucumber!" And your cousin Delores: "I haven't had a cucumber like that since I don't know when."

Everyone wants to take credit for these cukes. Your Germans will say these are German cukes. "But we don't add any paprika (sniff)." Your Bulgarians will say they're Bulgarian cukes. "My grandmother never added vinegar." Same goes for all these broads up and down the Danube—your Croats, your Serbs, your Romanians and just about anyone else who's lineage was one turn away from going Gypsy and who ever thought of brining a cucumber in order to give it that certain crispness.

I don't care about any of that. What you have here is the regular Hungarian Cucumber Salad (*uborka salata*) no matter what anybody else says. The only problem with this salad is that once you make it, everyone will ask you to make it all the time on account of it being "the best cucumber salad they ever ate," so you're standing at a point of no return. Do you or do you not want to be a slave to squeezing cukes for the rest of your life? Only you can decide. Don't make that decision based on account of my having crossed over to the other side years ago by way of Popiel's Dial-O-Matic and the blood coursing through my veins. You can see where it's got me.

Knowing When To Say When

I can't remember exactly when I began referring to my husband as the Goat, although it seems we'd been married at least 10 years. As previously noted, I will also call him by his last name only, particularly when the message is cautionary.

"Don't be an asshole, Nowjack."

My legal name is also Nowjack, as I was under the influence of my splendid king's myriad charms when we married and decided to change my name from the poetically Irish Erin O'Brien to the clunky and angular Erin Nowjack. When I began writing in earnest, however, I returned to my maiden name for those endeavors.

"I'll keep you, Nowjack, but your name has got to go."

To his credit, my dearly beloved did not protest the nominal change nor did I seek to legally return to O'Brien. A formal name change is a woeful prospect indeed that I do not care to revisit. When people ask me (with thinly veiled distrust since it is different from my husband's and lyrical to a fault) whether or not Erin O'Brien is my real name, I indignantly respond, "It sure as hell is! I was born with it, wasn't I? What? You want to see my birth certificate?"

I will sometimes call my husband "you warlock" when I do not wish to credit him for credit he is due. For instance, if he has bested me at Blokus, I narrow my gaze at him and say, "You warlock!" and thereby assign the win to some vague black magic at work behind the scenes.

But Goat remains as my favorite nickname and has bled into the more tender parts of our relationship.

"Want me to rub my boobies on your goat fur?"

"Okay!"

So it makes perfect sense that I found myself standing at the corner beer and wine store where the owner helps you pick out some Good Beer when your Good Beer friends are coming over and where they sell packages of beef jerky and pretzels from a jar (or at least they used too) and still have a rack in the rear of the store that houses skin rags (with plastic modesty cards obstructing the cover images), when I spied a funny bottle of wine called Goats do Roam, that I elected to purchase solely for that reason.

The Goat and I had a few laughs over the bottle and drank the goat wine with an otherwise unremarkable dinner. I regarded the empty bottle and, seeing as it was the reason I bought the wine to begin with and because I suffer from container disease (an affliction that compels me to save every empty Cool Whip, margarine and sour cream container until I have so many that nested stacks of them collapse under their own weight whenever I open the awkward corner-shaped bottom cupboard [contemptible in its own right due to the disparity between the copious space within the cabinet and the relatively small and oddly shaped opening that prohibits getting anything large into it] where I keep them), I decided to keep the goat bottle.

Although I deem it perfectly acceptable to keep thirteen empty Smart Balance containers (for which I have only six lids that I cannot find), I couldn't really keep an empty Goat wine bottle lying around. I didn't want to be misconstrued as the batty broad at the end of the street who saves droves of wine bottles on account of their goat labels. You start that and pretty soon, you're saving bottles because they're shaped like a cat or are made out of blue glass. And how far is the she-saves-cat-shaped bottles square from the land of "commemorative" items such as plates purchased via offers in the Sunday coupon circular that feature John Wayne, Marilyn Monroe or scenes from *The Wizard of Oz*? Not far enough (my commemorative Andy Warhol Campbell's tomato soup cans do not count).

So I had to fill the Goat bottle with something. Flowers? Decorative dried beans? Marbles? All of that was too pedestrian. I needed something less inert, something that stood on its own, even if from inside a goat bottle.

Something like jellybeans.

That I had actually fabricated a reason to buy jellybeans when the giant bunny wasn't due for months inflated me with joy. That fact, in conjunction with the singular purpose of the forthcoming purchase, moved me to elevate the entire project within the realm of jellybeanery. There was only one bean worthy of this job. So what if they were a little more expensive?

In no time, I was at the Jelly Belly self-serve kiosk in the gourmet grocery with kid in tow. I plucked an empty bag from the convenience rack and placed it under the tangerine chute. The darling little orange beans shwooshed into the bag with soft tinkles as I drew open the release lever. A satisfied smile spread across my face.

Juicy pear and peach. Lemon-lime and coconut. Red apple. I giggled and moved around this jolly paradise island.

My kid, unsure of how to handle what appeared to be a windfall of extraordinary proportion, tentatively asked, "Can we get some kiwi, Mom?"

"Sure!"

Very cherry and crushed pineapple and mango. I threw open the levers and let gravity do all the work.

"Isn't that enough?" said my daughter, eying the bulging bag.

"Move over," I said. "You're right in front of the

Buttered Popcorns." And so it went until the polite little zippered bag was full to bursting with an impolite volume of jellybeans.

At the checkout, a digital display informed me that I was obliged to pay over $20 for about two and a half pounds of jellybeans.

"Shit," I said, blinking at the glowing numbers.

"No swearing, Mom."

"Just don't tell your father," I said to her as I shelled out the green to the clerk and thought, *self, you are not going to pull a Clamato on these beans!*

It takes a big person to admit they love Clamato.

"You drink tomato and clam juice?" my friends say with disgust after I explain the crux of Clamato.

"Um, yeah," I mumble and look down.

Even Motts, the maker of Clamato, seems embarrassed by its product. The Clamato label features a glistening glass of red liquid along with some celery, tomatoes, lime and, tucked behind the glass and barely visible, an innocuous-looking clam shell, as if to say, *Hey, there's lots to love in here! Never mind that pesky clam.* Motts also doesn't like to own up to Clamato. The only place you'll find the maker's name is in tiny squeaking letters on the back label along with the mandatory address of origin and a grudging "product of USA."

In the world of foodstuffs, Clamato has a low ranking. It's like Spam's ugly step-sister. Those cute rectangular cans of Spam will occasionally be stacked in a we've-got-nothing-to-hide-here! display at the end of the aisle (and yes, I have been known to wash down Ritz crackers topped with Spam and a dash of Tabasco with a Stroh's beer; and yes, I did even once make Spam "sushi," which I proudly dubbed The Cleveland Roll). Dropping a can of Spam in your cart borders on kitschy. Buying a bottle of Clamato, however, is a closeted experience.

Grocery managers understand that we who enjoy Clamato like to do so discreetly. Think of an alky glancing over one shoulder then the other before fishing a flask from the murky depths of the cabinet under the sink and topping off their morning coffee. No one likes to be seen putting a bottle of Clamato in their cart. Hence, there is never, ever a Clamato display of any sort. No one can deal with Clamato. Not the makers, not the sellers, and least of all the consumers.

We Clamato drinkers don't like people watching us chew our nails as we fret over the "nutrition facts" on the label. And we'll pay any price, so you'll never see BOGO

(Buy One Get One!) under the four dusty Clamato bottles, which are usually on the top shelf of the juice aisle, between the Knudsen's Very Veggie and those dubious cans of Frank's Quality Kraut Juice.

Clamato might not be so bad if it were derived from fresh tomato juice and the actual broth that pours from the spigot of a huge blue and white-flecked enamel steamer pot that is sometimes denoted by the word CLAMS! in cursive letters.

The terrible truth about Clamato is that it's actually some combination of water, tomato concentrate, high fructose corn syrup, MSG, salt, citric acid, onion and garlic powders, celery seed, ascorbic acid "to maintain color" (I love that Mott's explains this ingredient, almost an apology: *Hey, we only put the ascorbic acid in there to keep this shit good and red.*), dried clam broth, spices, vinegar, natural flavors and red 40. *(Er ... about that last one, folks ... the tomatoes and ascorbic acid weren't quite doing the job so we went ahead and just added some of our regular red as well.)*

Eight ounces of Clamato contains 800 milligrams of sodium.

I tell myself every time that no one should drink anything that has 33 percent of the day's salt in one cup. What if I want a Cleveland roll later on? But one glass here and there, moderation and all that jazz, right? Thirty minutes on the elliptical will sweat that out, no problem.

With that intention (and while no one is looking), I pluck a stratified blood-red bottle of Clamato from the shelf and drop it into my cart while evoking an image of the next day's breakfast: a whole wheat bagel, fat-free cream cheese and a sensible six-ounce glass of Clamato garnished with a lemon wedge (never mind that I don't have a fresh lemon at home nor have I any intention of buying one). Call that a perfect send-off to the gym. What a good girl! I tell myself. Maybe I should buy a fresh tube of pink lipgloss as well ...

The day transpires in the usual way and soon enough I am a-slumber. The black space between 11 p.m. and 2 a.m. is populated with even sleep and soft dreams. But then come the nameless hours between 2 and 5 a.m. that bring the demons and desires, the sleepless fits. I toss and turn, thinking my unconnected and mostly useless thoughts: *A touch of gray ain't so bad, just ask the Grateful Dead. Dry-clean only does not necessarily mean dry-clean only. Tina Fey will be too old to play you by the time they get around to making a film version. Do not eff up.* So it goes until the image of the gleaming bottle of Clamato comes crashing in on all of it. I try to push it away to no avail. In no time, I am tiptoeing down the stairs, snickering to myself like a misplaced Grinch on his way to suck down the last can of Who Hash.

Nude save a pair of cotton undies, the miracle of the refrigerator light spills upon me. I wrap my hands around the bottle and shake, shake, shake, all my Erin flesh jiggling along in celebration.

I relish the twist of the cap. The sound of the breaking seal is barely audible, but satisfying nonetheless. I don't bother with a glass, just stand ablaze in the glorious illumination of the open refrigerator, guzzling the clammy, sweet, salty, tomatoey nectar. I cannot stop myself.

I. Fucking. Love. Clamato.

The next morning, I wake with the uncomfortable results of consuming 3,200 milligrams of sodium and 240 calories of what is essentially colored, flavored and diluted tomato concentrate and high fructose corn syrup. I slither to the breakfast table. My dearly beloved clears his throat with no further comment on my bloated appearance or the empty Clamato bottle on the counter.

"Never again," I vow in a throaty voice. "I'm never buying it again!"

Six months later, beads of sweat form on my upper lip as I peer up at the top shelf of the grocery juice aisle and reach up with a shaking hand.

###

There are other foodstuffs with which I cannot control myself. General Mills transformed the homemade and mostly wholesome concoction of Chex Party Mix, which contained understandable ingredients such as butter and Worcestershire sauce, into a prepackaged cheddar-flavored version that contains suspicious ingredients such as soy lecithin and distilled monoglycerides. Although I thoroughly enjoyed the original version and could eat it in appropriate amounts, the banal newfangled adaptation does precisely what all those chemicals are intended to do: strip me of will power. But where is the interest in that? Woman eats bag of cheddar flavored Chex Mix. So what?

Garlic frosting, on the other hand, is a food compulsion with infinitely more character. Garlic frosting (my nomenclature) is actually a garlic aioli that you can only buy at that one Dairy Deli across town that's owned by a Lebanese family. They swear they use only garlic, olive oil and salt to make the garlic frosting, impressive in its own right as the garlic frosting is just that—a rich creamy emulsion that you'd spread on cake if it wasn't the strongest garlic concoction imaginable.

I love it to a fault, shoveling it into my terrible self by way of anything I can find: bread chunks, pretzels, potato chips, raw vegetables, etc. During the entire garlic frosting orgy, I smell offensive in both breath and body. I battle the garlic odor by taking handfuls of breath capsules (the efficacy of which I am completely unsure) that are composed of parsley and sunflower seed oils.

My garlic frosting obsession is a lot like my Clamato addiction. I convince myself that moderation will prevail at the onset of the ordeal, wax lustfully ecstatic the moment consumption begins, find myself in a cloud of heady intoxication during said consumption, and feel at once relieved and shameful at its conclusion.

"Just say no!"

Yeah, right.

But really, should a person—just a regular person's person—harbor guilt for marrying a square of Belgium chocolate and a mini pretzel and placing the perfectly balanced saltysweet tidbit upon her tongue? It is at once rustic and European (subliminal inference: *this isn't snacking, it's practical applied sophistication*).

I shall not suffer persecution for having a jar (a huge jar) of whole salted pecans that my Aunt Dorothy rightfully purchased at Costco due to "a price you cannot believe" and gave to me ("what could one person possibly do with all these pecans?"). There is no shame in possessing a perfectly unremarkable carton of Dutch chocolate ice cream.

That a person should follow the obvious extrapolation from Belgium chocolate pretzel euphoria to salted pecan

Dutch chocolate discovery is only natural. (After all, the square of Belgium chocolate was a one-time only individually wrapped affair that I found while cleaning out my purse and this party isn't over yet, cannot be over yet. No, not yet.)

It is not a mistake to place the open jar (yawning open, gaping open, begging-to-be-penetrated open) of salted pecans upon the kitchen counter next to the open carton of Dutch chocolate ice cream. There is no wrongdoing when one extracts a spoon from the silverware drawer in order to construct just one spoonful of ice cream daintily garnished with just one gorgeously roasted pecan. This is, arguably, a god-given right.

And when I part my weary lips and insert said creation into my mouth, it is indeed divine, as are the second and third spoonfuls. This is the seraphic companion to the avant-garde chocolate pretzel.

The fourth spoonful of Dutch chocolate ice cream garnished with one salted pecan is the one that breaks through some virginal barrier. This fourth spoonful is every bit as delicious as numbers one through three, but I cannot deny that number four crosses a line and my new companions, however distant on the horizon, are sin and decadence.

With spoonful number five comes something even more ominous: a tiny bit of disappointment. I take that along as I endeavor onto spoonfuls six and seven, which are unfortunate mandates. With them, comes verbalization.

"Effing hell."

And disgust.

"No way did I just take one more scoop."

The thrill is gone and now I've got to get it back, which is how the bottle of maple syrup ends up on the counter next to the giant jar of salted pecans and the carton of Dutch chocolate ice cream. As I apply a glistening bead of syrup to yet one more pecan, I finally take the Lord's name in vain.

"Goddamnit anyway!"

Eventually but not soon enough, the spoonfuls lose their numbers. Their place in line no longer becomes notable or distinguishable. The orifice has been breached, repeatedly. We know each other in the biblical sense and everything old will not be new again. Wilted roses. Blanche and Streetcars. I chew with determination, a single tear sliding down my cheek.

As for the Jelly Bellies, they lasted at least a month. Well, maybe not a whole month.

The Great Porcine Offering

I vowed long ago never to drive a mini van and have since adhered to that pledge. Small, smart and sporty is a must for me as well as five on the floor (although someday I aspire to have a sixth gear). I am a gear-jamming purist. Why would I want some engineering jamoke over at Honda deciding what gear I should use as I maneuver across the purple mountain majesty? I love the feeling of torque, a good downshift turned gas guzzler by a simultaneous punch of throttle. Inclement weather notwithstanding, I almost always drive with all the windows open, the A. C. turned off and of course, blaring music. Although not the most comfortable way to drive, it imparts a certain credibility to transforming "I just drove through" to "Yeah, I've been there."

These practices are never more important than when a drive becomes a road trip. I detest the idea of traveling in a polite temperature controlled box, but doing so at high speed is the zenith of affable mediocrity. What's the point? Any good road trip is metaphysical as well as physical, but an Erin O'Brien road trip is a violent tumble through time, space, and life.

In my early thirties, I took such a trip with a friend. It was an extended and beautifully pointless jaunt from Cleveland, Ohio to Death Valley, California. When we arrived at our destination, I took a swig from a fresh bottle of Wild Turkey, poured the rest out in order to memorialize my brother who had committed suicide a few years before, and got back in the car to head home. We were as such, en route back to Cleveland on Interstate 80, when we crossed Nebraska and discovered that the Erin O'Brien-style road-trip, by its very nature, sometimes imparts more than "a certain credibility."

"Do you smell that?" I yelled over the whirring noise of the road. The speedometer was hovering around 80.

My associate yelled back, "I wasn't going to say anything until you said something." She was smoking, no small task with all that hot humid road air whipping around us.

"Hot balls, that stinks!" I screamed.

"Must be some sort of factory around here," she said. We were Cleveland girls. What else could create a stench such as this?

I eyed the flatness of Nebraska that stretched all around us. "No factory out here," I said. "Must be some sort of livestock."

"Cows?" she said.

"This smells different from the cows," I said. We'd had plenty of experience with them through Amarillo on the trip out (we had opted for Interstate 40 westbound).

"Wait!" I yelled. "What about pigs?"

"Like one of those gargantuan pig farm factories," she said. We sped on.

"Holy shit!" I said after several minutes. "It still stinks."

"It's like ... toxic," she said.

"Keep smoking," I said.

"I will."

On and on we drove as the vile odor lingered, thick and strong enough to nearly qualify as a taste.

Surely, that memory alone would be enough to convince me that it is a very bad idea indeed to put anything in your mouth that is sired and raised amid such a miasma. Surely, careening over that fetid stretch of rural highway was a seminal moment. Surely.

Oh, how I wish that were so; that my words right now would decry the deplorable pig factories and laud the good glowing art of responsible humane farming and environmentalism.

But I don't have one goddamn alibi, not one.

Because after those little piggies have been farmed, shipped, stunned, bled, scalded, eviscerated, split, cooled and butchered, they end up in a freezer bin on sale for $1.99 a pound. Perhaps that price is unremarkable at first blush, but when juxtaposed against a three-dollar six-ounce bag of spinach, which translates to EIGHT DOLLARS A POUND, or a $2.79 loaf of bread, or a $3.99 bag of chips, or the $10.99 bag of better coffee (a departure from the usual Maxwell House purchased in anticipation of a heavy writing week ahead–big treat, woot!), $1.99 a pound for any type of meat spells bargain galore.

A seven or eight pound loin at two bucks a pound means one or two meals of chops, at least a half dozen pulled pork sandwiches, and perhaps a small smoked pork roast. (The last being Goat-willing, of course. Smoking meat is a messy outdoor event that requires bricks, wood chips, water and fastidious tending for which I have no patience.)

With said realization clearly outlined in my mind, there I stand in the meat section as the familiar feeling of falling down washes over me. I sigh a great sad sigh for all the disappointed little piggy ghosts floating over the bin and dive in with an empty silk purse and a sow's ear full of guilt.

Oh, the maddening hypocrisy of it all.

Depending on what time of year it is, the very same bin will be filled with chunks of piggy yet again. But instead of grayish raw whole loins, the red-netted wonders take over:

ready-to-eat hams, full up with nitrates and sodium and "natural" flavoring. A 15-pounder may originate from the same ill-fated animal as the seven and a half pound loin, but that's where the similarities end. Because when these mothers go on sale, they really go on sale.

"Whole Semi-Boneless Hams, $0.99 per pound!"

Never was an exclamation point more appropriate, for this is the sign of change; although there are no options from which to choose. This quiets all the admonishing piggy voices from beyond. Despite the consternation on my face as I rummage through the deep refrigerated trough and think, *what the hell are we going to do with a whole ham?* the inevitable conclusion has already been drawn. How can I possibly not pay a dollar a pound for, well, anything, particularly something as dense and candid as a ham? Out go any remaining scraps of compassion for He Who Once Oinked and into my cart goes a giant pink wonder.

"Shit."

As I push it through *Your Quality Meats* (as denoted by two-foot tall lettering on the rear wall) and into the realm of *Farm Fresh Dairy* (identical lettering, a more dubious assertion), the ham grows and grows. By the time I reach *Baked Goods* (honest enough) the ham is as big as me—no, bigger than me. Or am I shrinking? By the time I glide past *Canned Fruit and Vegetables* (less gloriously asserted on a hanging placard), I am an inch-high micro Erin, pushing laboriously against the hard rubber wheel of my Wonder Cart, every bit the marvel of its namesake at Coney Island. The ham has also transformed, it is no longer a dull ovoid chunk of plastic-wrapped meat. It fills the monster cart. Pineapple discs, dotted in their middle with red red red maraschino cherries festoon the gargantuan ham's exterior. Fragrant smoke tendrils drift from the ham and transform into come-hither fingers, enticing all whom I pass. They turn and smile at this, the inception of a great American tradition: the Ham-a-thon.

Day 1

I heave the ham out of my car and haul it inside while thinking, *so this is what 15 pounds feels like*, (fifteen pounds being a constant operative in my life: the amount of weight I'd like to lose or the amount of weight I say I'd like to lose). I plop the ham onto the kitchen counter and back away, staring at it and breathing hard. The house is completely still.

"Damn."

The ham does not respond, just taunts me with its presence.

A brilliant idea dawns. I shall double my odds against

this behemoth right off the bat. I fly out to my husband's workbench and pluck a hacksaw from the pegboard, dislodging the metal pin from which it hangs. (This is what happens with every metal pin on the pegboard whenever I interact with it. As expected, the pin then clatters to the Land Of Things Never Retrieved behind the workbench. I push away the usual frustration in favor of the task at hand.) After a quick stop in the upstairs bathroom, wherein I sterilize the blade with rubbing alcohol and dry it with a tissue, I am back in the kitchen, putting saw to ham and enthusiastically cutting the monster in two, going straight through the bone with surprising ease. Yards of Saran wrap later and with the freezer as my accomplice, I have won fifty percent of the battle, at least for the time being.

Into the oven goes the ham, sans pineapple and cherries, which were really just figments in the preliminary reverie of my relationship with the ham. The business end of the seduction will release in an hour or so when the aroma of baked ham fills the house: reality's counterpart to the cartoon smoke fingers that followed me through the grocery.

I bustle about, furiously peeling potatoes and readying foodstuffs for a wholesome and economic family dinner. I bask in the righteousness of it all as I settle down to snap the green beans. This is our finest hour, our honeymoon: Erin + Ham = True Love. I have no intention of letting one bit of the happiness escape from the balloon.

That evening, intoxicated with my savvy, I heartily eat baked ham and scalloped potatoes, miles away from malodorous pig farms. My husband congratulates me again and again. "This is good ham!" he says. My daughter has a second helping. I smile.

I am a domestic phenom.

Day 2

"Don't you think scalloped potatoes are actually better the second day?" I ask and turn to my daughter. "Eat your ham, sweetheart."

Day 3

"Ham and waffles is such a treat!" I say perkily. "Honey, pass me the syrup."

Day 5

"Because we don't waste food, sweetie, that's why."

Day 6

My husband comes into the kitchen and sees the brown paper bag and apple that indicate I am making his lunch. He looks down as I carve away at the familiar pink carcass.

"How about one with butter and one with cheese?" I

ask, pulling the bread out.

He musters a stoic expression and levels his gaze out the window. "That's fine," he says, swallowing hard. "That sounds just fine."

Day 8

"Let's go out for burgers," offers my husband.

"What?" I bark with incredulity. "*Ham*burgers? Why would we do that when we've got this perfectly good ham here?"

My daughter creeps into the other room. I laugh maniacally and hack off a chunk of meat, pop it into my mouth. "See?" I say. "It's delicious! And are you forgetting that this ham cost us just pennies a serving?"

Day 11

Pasty white and with shallow breath, I pull the crusty ham heel from the fridge. With little attention to the trimming of fat or hardened rind, I cut it into pieces.

I screw the meat grinder attachment onto the ancient KitchenAid K4-B and turn it on low. One by one, the ham chunks go in. The process is strangely satisfying, even more so than the grinding of the raw beef. I have led my family through this journey one step at a time and this moment is earned. I drop grisly chunks of ham into the grinder's feed spout. The familiar wet squishing noises fill the kitchen.

The sinewy ham goes in the yawning spout; an homogenous pink foodstuff squeezes out through the production holes.

Beautiful.

I cut off the last possible scrap of ham and consider the oily white bone, with it's clinging threads of meat and fat. The fleeting thought of split pea soup races through my mind, but then I remember that the evil twin ham half is still in my freezer. I open the patio door to a blast of wintry air and hurl the bone into the backyard where it lands and tumbles end over end twice on the ground before succumbing to rest.

I remove the bowl of ground meat crumbs - the ham's last stand - from beneath the meat grinder and add an unceremonious dollop of mayonnaise.

I pour three fingers of whiskey into a glass, set it on the table. Out comes the red box of Ritz and the Tabasco. I set them next to the bowl of ham spread, a butter knife impaling the pink mass.

I knock back half of the whiskey. "Dinner's ready!" I bellow.

###

The story of porcine gifts does not end with a bowl of mayonnaise and sodium-rich ham that has been ground into submission. It started long before my snout ever inhaled the smell of the good earth and has yet to find its curly-tailed end. There is more to a pig than chops and roasts and ham spread sandwiches.

Although my Gram Soos was of German descent, she married into that big Hungarian family as well as its food traditions, many of which she kept after divorcing my grandfather. On Christmas morning, for example, when Gram arrived loaded with bags and baskets of gifts, she invariably had a covered tinfoil pie pan nestled somewhere within that housed the holiday *kocsonya*. We pronounced it kuch-en-ya.

Say *kocsonya* and, baby, you've just said *jellied pigs' feet*.

However challenging that concept may be, simply reading those words does not do the event justice. The shallow tin was filled with cooked pigs' feet congealed in aspic, which was essentially meat jelly that Gram made from the liquid in which she'd boiled the feet.

At some point during the course of the day, usually in the post gift-opening lull when everyone was perusing their booty, Dad would get a cold beer, the Tabasco sauce, and the tin of kocsonya. He'd pluck one of those mothers out of there; the act of which made a noise that I cannot sufficiently describe: just know it is the sound associated with a cooked pig's foot disengaging from a solid mass of meat jelly. Use your imagination.

Dad would dribble a bit of hot sauce on the pig foot chunk, from which bedraggled bits of meat jelly hung, put it in his mouth and hold onto it while he sucked off the aspic and chewed off the meat. Despite Dad's otherwise polite and careful eating habits, he could not execute the consumption of kocsonya without an unfortunate slurp noise or two slipping out. When the bone was picked clean, he'd set it aside on a plate or napkin and pluck out another piece. The whole operation was punctuated with slugs of beer.

Kocsonya is a dish with very low curb-appeal.

Despite that, the annual kocsonya affair was one of the fondest communications between Gram and her son-in-law, sort of an unspoken understanding. Neither my brother, my mom nor I ever ate any of it. Nonetheless, it is an indelible Christmas memory.

Recipes for kocsonya are not difficult to find. They are also simple in their execution. Although I know a butcher who would happily procure pigs' feet for me, I've never endeavored to make the dish. Hence, unless I wake up one day with a new leaf of kocsonya curiosity unfurling within, or find someone else who enjoys it (perhaps my daughter will marry a pigs' feet connoisseur just like her grandmother did), my Irish Hungarian family's traditional plate of jellied pig's feet on Christmas is liable to join the vast majority of my family in the sweet hereafter.

Farewell pigs' feet. Farewell chilled meat jelly. Farewell kocsonya.

But I just couldn't let that happen with the speck.

In college, I imagined myself a budding Holly Golightly. My attempts to emulate Audrey Hepburn's signature character from *Breakfast at Tiffany's* included using a cigarette holder and referring to dorm room beer bashes as "cocktail parties." The other coeds and I would substantiate that assertion by wearing dress gloves and serving martinis made from a five-dollar bottle of USA (U Save Alot) vodka during the soirees. I pined for Hepburn's sculpted hair, the dreamy fire escape, and (of course) the Givenchy gown and oversized glasses she wears in the opening scene of the movie. Most of all, I loved her unassuming sophistication as she nurses her otherwise inconsolable blues, which she dubs the "Mean Reds" with a sweet roll and coffee in front of the display windows at Tiffany's.

Eventually, I grew out of my *Breakfast at Tiffany's*

fantasy. After all, Cleveland is not New York and I am not Audrey Hepburn. I did, however, adopt one of Holly Golightly's habits, the one upon which the title is based. When I get the Mean Reds and I am suddenly afraid, but I don't know what I'm afraid of, I head for Cleveland's West Side Market, purchase one of Maha's falafel sandwiches (with hot sauce and hummus, please), and meander through the grid of vendor stalls, just like Clevelanders have been doing since 1840. I pass the cases of poultry and lamb and the one stall where there is always a whole baby pig displayed. The bakery stalls tempt me with their layered tortes and loaves of crusty Italian bread as I make my way to the West 25th Street entrance. Once there, I don't step out onto the street, but instead I turn left in the foyer and ascend the steps to the Market balcony. There I hop onto the stone ledge and watch all the action of the market unfold before me. Moms tug toddlers from trays of frosted cookies. Seniors wheel carts laden with parcels. A young woman points to the two chops in the back. Clerks pull pencils from behind their ears and scribble prices on white-paper packages. I chew my falafel and kick my legs. I sigh. My great grandfather Doubler traded his sweetcorn and potatoes here. Gram Soos used to treat me to delicious containers of freshly ground peanut butter from Rita's stand. This is where I belong and as long as I can come here and verify that, everything will be all right. Despite the fact that there is not a baby blue box tied with a white ribbon anywhere in sight, the Mean Reds secede.

When I finish, if the Hungarian is welling up in me proper, I amble over to Dohar's (the stall across from Ohio City Pasta, the one on your right if you're heading for the northernmost 25th Street door), because there are still remnants of Hunky in this town and I'm just the girl who knows where they are.

"Hey man," I say to the man with the thick hair and soiled apron, "You got any *szalonna*?" (Pronounced zuh-luh-na, full name: cigány szalonna; a smoked or paprika-cured Hungarian bacon.)

"Sure I got szalonna," he says. "How much you need?"

"Aw hell about a pound," I say. "A good fatty chunk—really fatty. I'm making speck."

"Speck!" blurts the man next to me. "Are you really making speck? Old-time speck?"

"Hell yes," I say.

"That's the best thing I've heard all day," he says, grinning widely and shaking his head. "Speck! She's making speck!"

Next it's Michael's Bakery and a righteous loaf of Jewish rye, then a stop at Kristi's Produce (stands 61 and 63—right in the corner of the produce arcade) for a big sweet Vidalia.

I head to the parking lot with my bootie in tow, the Mean Reds all but a memory. I flip open my cell and call Mom. "Why don't you come on over tonight and have some speck?"

"Speck!" she says. "You don't have to ask me twice."

You make Hungarian speck by scoring that chunk of szalonna in a waffle pattern, spearing it onto a good long barbecue fork and roasting it over an open fire until it starts to drip. Then you catch all those fat drippings on pieces of rye bread, top them with thin slices of onion, salt, pepper and paprika and that's it. Dad used to call speck "greasy bread."

At home, the four of us, Mom, Eric, Jessie and I, sit around the fire as Eric wields the szalonna.

"Here Mom," I say as I top off the first slice with the onion et al., "you take the first piece."

She bites into it. "Man, that's some good speck."

The fat goes back over the flame.

"Kid," I say to Jessie, "you've got to try some speck."

"Can I have mine without onion?"

"Sure, kid," I say. Concessions.

I prepare the next piece and hand it to my 11-year-old. To my surprise, she takes a big bite without grimacing, or complaining.

"This is pretty good," she says.

"Yeah?" I say, stunned.

"Yeah," she says. "Can I have another slice?"

"Well, dig the Hunky in you, kid," I say.

"What's 'Hunky?'" she asks.

"A rude word for Hungarian."

The scored surface of the szalonna eventually turns into tiny blackened crisps that I shave off. I cut new scores deeper into the chunk of fat.

"Those are the best part," says Mom.

Eric keeps up the roasting as I load up a piece of bread for myself, with plenty of onions and paprika and a sprinkle of those charred bits. I bite into my chunk of speck and close my eyes.

In my mind's eye, it's not just our party of four noshing on speck. Here the room is full of my people, my kin past and present. Here, my daughter isn't a sassy 11-year-old. She is just an infant bouncing and gurgling on my Gram Soos's lap.

"This kid?" says Gram, laughing, her body still lush and round, not yet shriveled and riddled with murderous cancer. "This kid is sort of a weird kid."

There's Gramp Soos, the sole source of my Hungarian blood, looking just as he did before divorce changed him forever in my eyes. I was ten when he swept my family from his life at the bequest of a new wife. He became a stranger after my bewildering heartache subsided. I would have mourned for this Gramp Soos instead of remaining dry-eyed when I heard of his death. But in my reverie, it's the real Gramp Soos standing by as he watches Dad pull the dripping szalonna from the fire.

"The next piece is for Erin!" he says.

Covering Dad's chest is his favorite blue and white striped turtleneck, underneath which his blood vigorously courses through an aorta that is still intact.

My brother John, having foregone any speck, is tearing a phonebook in half, his face twisted in a mock grimace of effort. He sets both halves down and winks at me. "The trick," he says, "is to start with just a few pages—then whatever you do, don't stop." He drains his beer can and sets it on the floor in preparation for his next parlor trick.

He positions one foot atop the can. Wobbling with careful balance, he stands precariously, slightly bent at the hips with his arms outstretched and his free foot floating behind him until he gets stability. He is an overgrown Karate Kid for a moment or two before he slowly, slowly, slowly crouches down and taps the side of the can oh-so-gently. It collapses instantaneously beneath his foot and somehow he does not fall.

Johnny triumphantly holds up the result of his effort—a perfect aluminum disc, before sneaking off for another belt of Wild Turkey. His handgun, the final shot from which whispered *suicide*, is nowhere in sight.

And there's Gram O'Brien lighting each of five wicks centered in a massive candle. It is a foot in diameter and just as tall, molded from deep purple wax. There is a cathedral of candles around her, short and squat, tall and thin, rose and lavender and periwinkle. Gram's made every one of them in her fascinating craft-laboratory, housed in the garage. Her features are beautiful and radiant above the glow, not yet twisted by the ravages of Alzheimer's.

Gramp O'Brien is holding court next to the makeshift bar on the kitchen table, telling the story of how he got duped into buying a fur coat for his new bride in 1935, only to find out it had been fashioned from the hide of a German Shepherd. The recollection has not yet been silenced by dementia.

My strapping cousin Jeff—my age—is guffawing under his shock of red hair. "Who wants to arm wrestle?" he booms then swigs from a bottle of Budweiser. His heart is still pumping, safe from complications of a drug and alcohol overdose that would stop its beating just before his thirty-fourth birthday.

Great Grandma Doubler is rocking back and forth, a short finger of Southern Comfort in the glass at her elbow. She's telling me about baking bread in a wood-burning stove, about fields of lily of the valley. Then she bends down and turns up the hem of her dress. "She this?" she says of the International Ladies' Garment Workers' Union label. "Always look for that label. I worked for the Union for years." I promise to comply.

She smiles, nods, then calls after great Gramp Doubler, *"Fred? Fred!"*

I open my eyes, misty from the daydream. Everyone is gone save my husband, mother and daughter here in this humble house. I take another bite of the rich speck, let the heat of the onion rise up through my nose and sting my eyes.

"Are you crying, Mom?" asks my kid.

"It's just the onions, baby," I say, thinking, *I have everything. I have everything.*

Part Two: To Have and To Hold

Husband and Wife

"How come everything I say is wrong?" Husband.

"It's not that everything you say is wrong," Wife. "It's that everything you say is wrong."

"But that's what I just said," Husband.

"No it's not," Wife. "You said, 'How come everything I say is wrong?'"

"Right," Husband.

"Wrong," Wife.

Going to the Chapel

Diamonds and daisies. Perfect sugar roses on the three-tiered wedding cake. *Bride* magazine and downtown "trunk" shows. Pretty girls tittering over trousseau recommendations and sipping flutes of champagne.

Lovely images? Perhaps. But all of it spells delusion to me. I want to shout at those little girls, *Why are you so worried about one day when you should be worried about the "till death do you part" portion of the proceedings?*

That said, a bride's relentless quest for a fairy-tale wedding never fails to fascinate me. There is a reality show that I cannot peel my eyes from whenever the remote leads me to it: "Say Yes to the Dress" chronicles the dramas of maidens in search of their perfect wedding gown as they unfold in the famed Kleinfeld Bridal Salon in New York City.

On "Say Yes to the Dress", I learn about things that were previously as foreign and mysterious to me as the secret rites performed by the Skull and Bones society of Yale/George W. and George H. W. fame. Behold the world of A-lines and veil fittings and bodices. There are empires, brocades and mermaid trains (Wait a second, did she say veil fitting?) Pouty brides and overbearing mothers stress and argue over it all. Every episode is full up with tears, terrors and hugs. One of my favorite installments featured a "blow-out" sales event with a running of the brides that rivaled the San Fermín festival in Pamplona. The show used to open with teaser lines.

"The most special day of your life."

"Sometimes it's harder to commit to the dress than it is to the fiancé!"

"What happens to the $11,000 dress after the wedding falls through?"

I'll tell you exactly what happens: some guy weeps with ecstatic joy after he realizes he's just been freed from a life-long emasculation served up by some silly little broad that would spend eleven grand on one fucking dress.

Although you could shriek the much-repeated mantra "A wedding lasts just one day, but a marriage is for life" at the top of your lungs to all the starry-eyed brides again and again and again, very few of them would hear you. So instead of bellowing a cliché, I'll illustrate my point with a few specific examples everyone can understand.

There are things no one tells you, little girl, as you're agonizing over fondant or buttercream. (My own wedding celebration, an understated affair held in my parent's home, did not include any cake at all, but instead, a modest selection of pastries. At no time did I regret the decision to forgo a three-tiered vanilla butter cake with candied ginger buttercream frosting done in a retro Peter Max inspired "Love" theme with tiny iridescent sugar beads in contrasting colors along the rims of each layer with an explosion of frosting "rays" emanating along the sides of the bottom tier [done in classic Maxian gradually changing colors] and with two discrete butterflies on top of the cake in lieu of traditional bride/groom figurines. No, I never thought twice about it.) Since not every surprise is a good surprise, oh darling bridelet, I'll fill you in on some things you should know before you go in, starting underneath it all.

Although you might believe that nothing lasts forever but the Earth and sea, your new husband believes that nothing lasts forever but the Earth and sea—and his underwear. Right now, the sight of his tighty-whiteys makes you giggle and want to play Naughty Spank Time, but you're closer to this scene than you think:

You're standing in the laundry room, one hand on hip, the other dangling a ragged tangle of cotton and elastic before your virile groom. "What exactly," you will say with an accusatory tone, "is this?" although you know perfectly well what it is.

"My underwear," he will say.

"This," you will boom with authority, "is not underwear." Then you will offer a dramatic pause as you huff and stare pointedly at the object of your discussion. "This is a group of fibers that once collectively dreamt it was a pair of underwear!"

"Maybe," he will say, "but it's also my favorite pair of underwear." Then he will shuffle off to the garage, leaving you at an impasse: Do you throw the blessed bundle away and suffer the consequences, or toss it in the washing machine so it may live to ride again? Don't answer too quickly. How would you like it if he made the executive decision to rid your top drawer of all your utility-grade grannie-style bloomers?

Now for a bonus hint: Since most heterosexual men are not capable of purchasing clothing, you're going to be buying his underwear for the whole happily-ever-after, so save yourself some cold truth and only buy him black skivvies. Don't ask any questions, just trust me on this.

Seeing as we're pretty close to the toilet, let's talk about the bathroom. The point about him turning it into a reading room has been belabored by many who came before me, so I'll leave that alone (and yes, it is a fact). Instead here is something you will not expect. Not long after I vowed to have and to hold, I noticed that the bathroom mirror was collecting dots of white foam at an alarming rate. The walls were amassing them as well, as were the vanity doors. Since there is no naturally occurring bathroom activity that produces such results, I've formulated the following ritual theory, the actual practice of which has never been captured on film:

The male of the Married Human Species starts with an inordinate amount of toothpaste. Next is überbrush. Brush brush brush brush brush! He brushes until his mouth is filled to capacity with foam. Then, in order to distribute this wondrous bathroom byproduct of which he is obviously proud, he opens his mouth and exhales slightly while moving his head back and forth in front of the mirror, the shower door, and the ceiling, thereby marking the entire room. Perhaps it's a territorial thing, like the pile of *Sports Illustrateds* on top of the toilet tank to which I previously eluded.

This next evil phenomenon ensues shortly after your visions of spending the entire night slumbering like two nude human spoons, cradled and peaceful, evaporate along with the bubbles in your honeymoon mimosas: Welcome to the long sleepless night, during which you flop around like a giant mudskipper as you brood over whether or not to throw away his terrifying underwear and pine for the simplicity of decisions such as fondant vs. buttercream. You're sweaty and uncomfortable. You stick your foot out of the covers because it's too hot and retract it two minutes later when it gets too cold. The glowing green segments on your bedside clock give way to one minute after another after another.

Because Life Is Not Fair, your husband is sleeping like a cadaver. Despite your huffing, blanket twisting and endless quest for the cool side of the pillow, he doesn't move, save the steady rise and fall of his chest.

Eventually, the magic moment arrives. The image of the toothpaste foam blobs morphs into one of happy polka dots. Your body settles perfectly into your blankie nest. That tingly sensation of impending sleep washes over you as your brain releases a lovely dose of melatonin. Just when you begin to drift into a dream of blue skies and crystalline contrails, an involuntary spasm shocks through your wrist—a sure sign that sleep is imminent, that's when it happens.

The man you married (on purpose) begins a slow shifting turn, often accompanied by a deep gutteral breath or half snore (in order to further indicate the profound restfulness of his slumber). Sure, it seems harmless, until you realize that the miserable warlock is slathered with a mysterious substance that is odorless, tasteless and unde-tectable by touch. I call it bed linen adhesive. It adheres the sheets and blankets to his furry chest and PJ pants. And as he rolls, he takes the portions covering you along with him and they drag maddeningly across your just-settled body.

Whether you yank the sheet back and bark, "Goddamnit!" or scrunch up your legs and plant your feet on his back in order to push him off the bed, it matters not. The blankie nest, the melatonin, the sky dream, it's all shit-canned. And you only have a half hour before the alarm goes off.

Something old, something new, something borrowed something blue?

Something my ass. This is what married life really looks like.

The Promiscuity Quotient

Before I walked down the aisle to join my splendid king until death do us part, I kissed my share of frogs (and I'm giving "kissed" a pretty broad definition). When my dearly beloved asked about the exact number associated with "my share," I gave him a completely accurate answer.

"More than one," I said, "and less than a hundred." Why belabor specifics?

"So who was the other guy?" asked my husband. You've got to give the guy points for being an optimist.

The actual number of men in a woman's past is just that—a number. And like her weight or age, numbers can be touchy. Kudos to the chaste damsels among us who can righteously assert that they have only shared the bed of one man who respectfully deflowered her on their wedding night and will grace her side for all eternity in the side-by-side plot already chosen at Memorial Acres. Some of us weren't so perfect.

During my adult single years, I worked as a staff

engineer for BP Oil, a job that frequently had me flying the friendly skies. I lived in a walk-up brownstone apartment that was about two miles south of my childhood home, where my parents still lived. My building and those surrounding it were populated by a bevy of chicks that looked just like me, with jobs and purses from Coach and two-door coupes. One of my closest associates lived in the brownstone next door.

When I wasn't traveling o'er the fruited plain, we chicks, in groups of two, three, or four, would often confer after work upon the front steps of my building (weather permitting), sipping cold beer, dragging on Marlboros and swinging our bare calves upon the hinges of crossed knees. We discussed our conquests in meticulous detail.

"It was bent."

"Bent?"

"To like, one side."

"I've never seen a bent one."

"Yep, it was bent to one side and it smelled funny."

"Funny?"

"It smelled sort of like peanut butter."

There were the men we had gone to bed with; the men we wanted to go to bed with; the men we might go to bed with; the men we couldn't quite remember whether or not we actually did go to bed with; and of course, the men we wished we'd never gone to bed with.

"He walks out of the bathroom wearing this thong underwear with an elephant head in the front that's got this little sleeve where his dinker's supposed to go that's supposed to be the elephant's trunk."

"Was his schwantz in the sleeve trunk thing?"

"I guess."

"What do you mean, 'guess?' Couldn't you tell if it was in there?"

"Not really."

"Jeez."

We'd talk about the men we couldn't imagine anyone going to bed with, which men were surprising, which were disappointing, which were unremarkable, and which were ridiculous. We'd deconstruct all the supporting evidence, whatever the assertion.

"He kept saying, 'Pull my titties! Pull my titties!'"

"I would have laughed. Did you laugh?"

"Yeah I laughed."

"What did he do? When you laughed?"

"Nothing. He just kept saying it."

"You might want to keep a close watch on your underwear drawer when he's around."

I imagine we were a pleasant fixture to the rest of the neighborhood, the attractive group of twentysomething women with our dangling cigarettes and cans of Budweiser, laughing on the stoop. When Richard (2b) or Matt (3a) would approach, the discussion would come to a dead stop and we'd part the way for him, our respective paired knees pointing towards either edge of the stone steps. The gent would bound up the stairs, our chants of "Hey Richard," or, "Hey Matt," floating in the wake of his energy and greeting of, "Afternoon, ladies."

Old Man Jim was the only man brave enough to linger at our party. From the moment the snow melted to the moment it blanketed the grass, Old Man Jim wore the exact same outfit: a lipstick-tube Speedo and cowboy boots. He was bald and continually sunburnt to a crispy-crisp. He drove a purple 1972 AMC Javelin, which was always parked directly in front of the stoop where we gathered. He was the "super" for the building next door.

"Hey Jim, you want a beer?"

"Why ladies," he'd say, pulling the gnawed stogie from the corner of his mouth, "I don't mind if I do." A collection of white whiskers sprouted from his chin.

Whenever Jim joined us, the conversation became uncharacteristically polite. We'd discuss the weather, the status of neighborhood lawns, or our cars.

"Look's like it's about time to mow again."

"Yep."

I can't recall Jim ever swearing or making a pass at any one of us. Fashion sense notwithstanding, he was a reed of civility amid our otherwise wooly collection of thistle.

"How's that Javelin running for you?"

"Smooth as silk."

Sometimes Jim would bring his own beer, usually a quart bottle of Pabst or Genny Cream Ale, which pretty much says it all. He may have brought around beers for us once in a while. I don't remember. Beer was a community resource. Everyone contributed and everyone withdrew. No one kept tabs.

When Jim's beer came to an end, a lull would ensue and he would sniff, reinstall the stogie in his mouth and excuse himself.

"Can't get started until you get started," he'd say, heaving himself from the step.

"Seeya Jim."

Jim would shuffle off in his cowboy boots and Speedo and our dubious conversation would resume, with the most personal topics reserved for the smallest groups.

"I counted," I said to one of my associates on a fair June day.

"You what?" she said. It was just the two of us.

"I counted," I said, exhaling and positioning my elbows upon the step behind me.

"No you didn't," she said.

"I counted," I said.

"No!" she barked. "Never happened. Forget it. You didn't."

"I counted." I said.

"No you didn't. It's against the law," she said, raising her beer to her lips. He arm stopped midway and her eyes shifted over to me. "You didn't write anything down, did you?"

"Well ... "

"Do not tell me that!" she said, slamming her beer down on the sandstone ledge. "You never count and you never write anything down. You have to destroy all evidence of this immediately if not sooner."

"But it was just a personal thing," I said. "A personal reference sort of thing."

"Personal reference my ass," she said. "If it's some sick, twisted curiosity inside of you, fine. But for chrissake don't count. If you have to quantify it, go and figure your promiscuity quotient."

"My promiscuity quotient?"

"Your promiscuity quotient," she said.

"Sounds complicated," I said.

"Nahhh," she said with a throw away gesture. "It's easy. First, you figure when you lost your virginity. Then count how many months since then."

"This is already too hard."

"All of these are estimates, nothing concrete," she said in a cautionary tone. "You're estimating—not counting. It's a big difference. Everything here is round figures. So figure your months and then the guys."

"The number of guys I zocked?"

"Right," she said, "but don't go saying 'zocked' or anything out loud. You're just estimating the number of guys. That's all the detail anyone needs."

"And how is that different from counting the number of lays?" I asked.

"It just is. For starters, we're talking a round number, give or take say," she hesitated for a moment, "say ... ten?" She looked at me for confirmation. I offered a barely perceptible nod. She continued, "An estimate accurate to ten. That's what it is. And you want to low-ball it."

"I need a scratch pad."

"No scratch pad," she said. "You can't write anything down. Just do it in your head."

"Okay then," I said. "But I'm losing accuracy."

"Good. Now take the estimate and divide it by the number of months you figured before," she says.

"No," I said.

"No what?" she said.

"I can't do that sort of division in my head. I need a calculator."

"Oh, all right already," she said. "Go on and get your calculator. Grab me another beer while you're up there."

I went through the wood and glass door that we'd propped open with a brick against the automatic lock and trudged up the stairs that still sported the building's original carpeting (circa 1928). It was festooned with garlands of red roses and had a unique 60-year-old carpet smell, but it was so old-fashioned that I loved it just the same.

In my apartment, I rifled through the clutter of my dainty lady's desk (gifted to me by Gram Soos when I was just a tot), swung by the small and ancient fridge (the freezer of which was not frost free and would accumulate so many inches of ice upon its dull aluminum walls that about the only thing that would fit in it was one half of a banana twin pop), and returned to the stoop with two fresh beers and the calculator.

"Here," I said, handing her one. I sat down, cracked my Bud Light, fired up another Marlboro and punched in the numbers. "Okay," I said. "It's-"

"NO!" she cried. "Don't tell me! You're not supposed to tell anyone.

"This is it? I looked back at the calculator.

"That's it," she said. "That's your Promiscuity Quotient—you're PQ. As long as it's less than one, you're fine."

"Why one?" I ask.

"Who could blame you for getting laid once a month?"

We nodded smugly. "But what if it's more than one?" I asked before quickly adding, "Not that mine's more than one or anything like that."

"Of course it isn't," she said. "But in such a rare instance—which neither of us will ever have to worry about—you just round-down. Or recalculate your estimate. Or you can forget the whole thing, wait ten years and do it again."

"Ten years?" I said.

"Theoretically the PQ will go down over time," she said. "Particularly if you get married. In the case of your marrieds, the estimate shouldn't go up that much in the course of ten years, right?"

"Right."

"But the number of months will increase by 120. Numerator and denominator—grade school stuff. Remember?"

"Sure. Smaller on top, bigger on the bottom. Gets you closer to zero." I said.

"Exactly," she said and we both paused and looked out over at a group of kids swinging on the jungle gym in the school playground across the street.

"Hey," said my associate, peering into the empty sleeve of her Marlboro pack. "I'm out of cigarettes. You got cigarettes. Let me have one of your cigarettes."

###

Having now been married nearly 20 years, my Promiscuity Quotient has indeed plummeted, although the sex is a far sight better and more regular than the sloppy conquests of my salad days. Not long after my dearly beloved asked about the men in my past, my associate called me to tell me that Old Man Jim, with his purple Javelin and boots and chewed up stogie and whiskers, had somehow shocked or offended one or more of the residents of the building he tended on account of his Speedo. They complained to the landlord, who insisted Jim wear outfits that covered more of his burnt brown skin.

He complied, and died about a year later.

Finding Mr. Right

Once while working at a downtown lunch joint during summer break from college, I encountered a singular Prince. He was seated at the head of the table with ten or so other suited businessmen. They were celebrating something with plenty of cigars and Manhattans. The Prince (a misnomer perhaps, he was about 50) beckoned me with a hooked index finger.

"C'mere, c'mere," he said. "Gotta joke for you."

I plastered on a smile and approached the table.

"C'mon, c'mon. Sit here in my lap."

Oh how I wish the Erin I am now had been there to stop the Erin I was then. But this Erin was not there and that Erin, interested in a fat tip, gingerly perched herself in the lap of the Prince.

"Now close your eyes," he said.

"I don't want to close my eyes," I said. It was getting more and more difficult to maintain the flirty façade. "What are you going to do?"

"I not going to do anything," he said. "Promise. Just

c'mon and close your eyes."

I did.

"Now imagine I'm holding a Barbie doll," he said, his boozy breath repelling me. "Point to where you think the top of her head is."

I did.

"Okay," he said. "Now point to where you think her feet are."

I did, although that Erin found the whole thing as disagreeable as this Erin.

"Now," he said with a rheumy giggle, "I want you to point to where her hoochy-coochy is." A collective chortle rose from the table.

Sadly, I was already beyond the point of no return. And when I extended my finger to the approximate center of the imaginary Barbie doll, the Prince promptly wrapped his wet lips around it.

I recoiled and jumped off his lap as all of his cohorts burst into hysterics.

I do not recall the remainder of my reaction. I probably offered a mirthless "heh heh" as I considered the contaminated state of my finger. Whatever I did, that performance as well as my associated service throughout the afternoon earned me an $18 tip on a $145 bill, which I do remember. The tip was strewn about the table, two fives and a flurry of ones, amid the ash- and butt-littered plates and smeared

12-ounce glasses that housed that watery remains of "Steamship" cocktails (for which the establishment was known).

Although I harbored no attraction to the Prince and his compadres, I offer this egregious example of assholiness by way of introduction. Behold the ten most important words to obey when interviewing prospective mates: Watch how he treats the waitress before you marry him.

I cannot properly credit that genius line as I do not remember where I heard it or read it. In fact, I didn't field it until after I was married. Instead of having that concise directive at the onset of my maiden years (as illustrated above), I had to figure it out the hard way. And even if I had had the ten-word litmus test, I'm not sure it would have saved me all that much frog-kissing. Sometimes you have to take the long way home.

Kissy kissy kissy!

That said, I have never met anyone who does not accurately project their entire self—past, present, future, inner and outer—whilst seated at a linen covered table, ratty barstool or even when driving through the Golden Arches. Being served food peels back a layer, something about the carnal need for nourishment butting up against the human idiosyncrasy of being served same and how it is rooted in our maternal past as well as class designation. This phenomenon's simplest permutation separates people into two categories: 1) Those who expect service and; 2) Those who appreciate it. You want a mate that hails from the latter camp.

The Prince was, incidentally, wearing a wedding ring, which does not necessarily mean his golden bride stuck her finger into an imaginary Barbie vagina before trotting down the aisle. But I'm betting there was something somewhere in their courtship that indicated the depth of her groom's repulsive nature—a paltry fifty cents left on the bar, change from the cost of two or three generous highballs served up with a smile and a white cocktail napkin; or a valet admonished before he was even allowed to complete his task: "The only thing you need to touch, champ, is the steering wheel. Do we understand each other?"

Here's another easy-to-understand example that sheds light on this nuanced mate-selection litmus test:

You're catching a late lunch with the group from the training seminar. It's 2 p.m., but the diner is still busy. Everyone is starving. The shelf beneath the heat lamp is loaded with plates. People are calling for the frazzled waitress with the dishes lined up her arm. "Miss?" they say with irritation as she brushes the hair from her eyes. Her polyester uniform is stained and her shoes are like the ones your Aunt Phyllis wears. Your droopy sandwiches arrive after a half-hour wait and the coffee needs refilling.

This is no time to worry about whether or not your

pickled turnips are wrapped snugly in your falafel sandwich or served in a plastic cup on the side. It's time to
watch and learn, babygirl.

Brad from Materials Management flips over the top of
his Special Grill Sandwich, lets out a barely audible sigh
and says under his breath, "I did not want lettuce. And what
about my mustard?"

It's the little things you're looking for: *my* mustard.

Instead of picking off the piece of lettuce himself and
employing the yellow barrel-shaped bottle of Plochman's
that's seven inches from his plate, Brad from Materials
Management beckons the waitress with a hooked finger.

"Miss?" he says tightly even though she's setting
a cup of coffee upon the table next to yours. When she
turns to see, he employs a controlled voice and explains
his dissatisfaction with his sandwich. And as the waitress
picks up his plate and recedes from the table, he shakes
his head and says with a pinched smile, "You just have to
explain yourself to these people."

These people.

Mark from the Columbus office, however, is ignoring
Brad and sort of grinning at you and chewing on his BLT.
The lettuce is wilted and the bacon is sparse. "How's the
BLT?" you ask.

"Terrible," says Mark without taking his eyes from
you. "Who cares?"

Now, which of these two guys is going to make a stink over separate checks? Which one is going to discreetly slip a few extra bills under the sugar bowl?

There you go.

That lunch trumps every single thing Brad from Materials Management might have to offer: money, a lakeside condominium, good looks. It negates roses. It even steamrollers his sexy little BMW Z4 Roadster and a member that's rumored to rival Rubirosa's (but even I admit that turning down a spin in the Beemer would be tough, let alone the member: a girl's only got so much will power).

To those little broads who read that last paragraph and sniffed, looked down or did anything else to indicate that a bit of rude behavior towards an incompetent dishrag of a waitress isn't all that bad, I say this: Lining your bed with diamonds, babygirl, won't keep you warm.

The waitress test is only the beginning. You have to pay attention. So what if a guy watches a little online porn? Everyone is entitled to a computer flesh fest once in a while. But if he has gold card membership to hoes. com, Her1stAnal.com and hogtied.com, this does not bode well. And yes, sensitivity does count, but if the guy in the cubicle next to you spends hours talking with his girlfriend about her menstruation cycle ("Is it light or heavy? Are we talking spotting?") without even lowering his voice, I suggest you decline his offer for coffee when they break up.

(Because, if you don't, you might end up gulping down a cup of joe as fast as you can while he sits opposite you practicing whatever habit modern day Romeos have replaced with smoking and saying, "You realize that everyone in the office will be talking about this, don't you? You and me? Having coffee? You realize they're probably talking already, the way we walked out together and everything?" his mustache a constantly moving punctuation mark as he pshaws, chats, sucks on his Newport and daintily laugh/coughs. Not that I know this from personal experience or anything.)

What a man drives is almost as indicative as how he tips. And I do not use the "almost" modifier lightly in that sentence. The how's-your-period-going-guy is likely to drive something nondescript, say a Taurus or a Focus, or, if, say, you were dating back in the late 80s, maybe he'd be in a vapid Dodge Aries K (again, not that I know for sure), just like a million other regular not-worried-about-your-monthly-flow other guys were back then. This is a case-by-case situation.

A car may be a pure extension of its owner.

Jack was a hockey player at Ohio University, as hard on his 1976 Plymouth Volaré as he was on the ice. The Volaré's finish was a dull primer gray with plenty of dings. The interior tan leatherette was torn and dimpled with cigarette burns.

During my freshman year (1983/84), Jack's car somehow kept sputtering along despite its abusive owner. The crowning moment for the Volaré was an ill-begotten trip from Athens to Dayton. Unremarkable at first blush, yes. But when Jack and his buddy Joe donned goggles (safety first!) and piled into the Volaré, it garnered my respect. The car had no windshield by then. They made it about 75 miles before the mission was terminated by one of Ohio's law enforcement representatives.

I laud any woman that takes on the challenge of a man like Jack, as long as she knows what she's getting into—a furious, dangerous and satisfying ride. She can probably expect to be a bit worn out when she slides down the exit tube.

Next consider the Lincoln Town Car. The spotless late-year model is driven by your uncle Frank, who wears a plaid fedora hat (always when he's driving and at no other time). And although he's had the same London Fog over-coat (and underlying physique) for 35 years, he purchases a new Town Car every three years on the Saturday after Thanksgiving. The majority of each Lincoln's mileage is garnered on Interstates 77 and 95 as Uncle Frank and Aunt Liz travel from Cleveland to Tampa on the first Thursday after Thanksgiving (except for that one year when the new Lincoln wasn't ready yet and they had to delay the trip one week) and from Tampa to Cleveland on April Fool's Day.

Aunt Liz knew exactly what she was getting when she first situated herself in Uncle Frank's 1981 Lincoln Town Car after he stepped into the Steno Pool and asked her out to lunch. At the Park Center Grille, they noshed on grilled ham and cheese with potato salad and a pickle spear, (him) and the Waist Watcher Platter (her), which consisted of a beef patty, a scoop of cottage cheese and a one half cup serving of fruit salad that came from a can and included not one, but two maraschino cherries (considered a lucky sign by Aunt Liz). By the time they got to the bottom of their bottomless glasses of iced tea, they knew that they would spend the rest of their lives together.

Conversely, Uncle Frank's first Town Car, a 1978 Continental model, is in the hands of its seventh owner, Cringe O'Dell, who lives in a trailer in Meigs County and does not think vegetable juice when he thinks V-8. He sports a collection of tattoos commonly referred to as a "sleeve" and is currently convalescing from a gunshot wound to the leg courtesy of his former roommate, Elk.

"Effing Connies are the best beaters," is the sort of thing Cringe says as he lights up a Winston. "Hey man, you wanna Blatz?"

Is there any question regarding the status of Cringe's fingernails? And if you had to guess whether he prefers ladies with deep cleavage over those with tiny twins, would it really be a guess?

But we understand Cringe. We understand the type of woman he will cast as Mrs. O'Dell. She will likely be a lovely bride all a-shimmer in a Lycra gown festooned with multi-colored sequins, replete with elaborate headpiece. May wedded bliss be theirs forever after.

I would be leery of a single man with no children who drives a minivan, which is completely unjustified and prejudicial, but that's how I feel.

Guys driving a gleaming F450 Super Duty with an immaculate empty bed liner take more than they need. Conversely, the man in the muddy Toyota Tacoma with its fringe of rust and bed full of tools and Lucinda Williams crooning on the box is worth a second look. I recommend utility grade over high maintenance. Every. Single. Time.

When I met my own splendid king, he drove a black 1990 Chevrolet Baretta GT. I was tooling around in a Red 1986 Honda Civic CRX. And as I previously stated, there are exceptions to every rule including the car rule (my dad was not well represented by the 1973 powder blue Ford Pinto or the faux wood-clad 1977 Cutlass Vista Cruiser station wagon, both of which were purchased used) and the waitress rule (even though I said there are exceptions to every rule, I cannot think of one exception to this rule), the CRX and Baretta represented Erin O'Brien and Eric Nowjack fairly accurately at that juncture in our lives.

Before the CRX, I owned two cars, both VW Beetles.

The first car was a '71 ($200) with an interior that smelled mysteriously of rotting flesh courtesy of a heater that would not turn off. In the summer of 1981, I drove it for two weeks as the heat blasted uncontrollably before the car mercifully threw a rod and died. ("Threw a rod" was my father's assessment at the time. I did not know what it meant then or now, but have always thought that saying the '71 Bug "threw a rod" imbued me with a certain tomboyish quality that I do not organically possess). My second bug ($500) had longer staying power. I drove it throughout my senior year at Lakewood High, undaunted by the passenger door that would fly open during enthusiastic left turns and the way the brake pedal would sometimes stick (a malfunction I remedied by tying a rope around the pedal, which I would pull up whenever it got stuck after I applied the brakes).

The bumble-bee yellow bug was not just tangibly diverse in its operation, it also provided more than one mode of transportation. I would gloriously race down the North-South residential streets that divided Lakewood into neat rectangular parcels and, using the local railroad crossings as launch pads, I'd get the yellow bug airborne, if only for a moment.

"Weeee!"

The Baretta signified a major shift in vehicles for Nowjack. That car entered his life six months before I did ("If you had seen my last car, you never would have dated me"). Prior to that, Nowjack helmed road-boats of the 1970s and early 80s: a Plymouth Fury ("the speedometer didn't work"), a car he cannot remember, a Chrysler Newport, a Buick Regal (the driver's side door didn't open"), and an Olds Delta 88 ("now that one had power windows"). But in 1990, having reached the age of 33, he decided to move on and purchase a brand new car.

The Baretta was competent, solid and reliable. My Honda was fast and small and tough, purchased used but in good condition. It was bright red with a sunroof, two seats and a hatch back. Black and red are perfect together.

And there was the way Eric Nowjack called me Irish and the way my big jealous tomcat Al mewed affectionately and weaved through his legs upon their first meeting. There was the way he reached down with his enormous hands and petted the cat so gently and the way Al responded by burrowing his face in Nowjack's palm.

And he didn't hold onto his money too tightly, nor did he make a big show of spending it.

And if there was only one cold beer left in the fridge, he'd hand it to you and pluck a warm Stroh's from the freshly purchased 12-pack the corner store guy had sold him apologetically as the power had been out all night and the better part of the day and he was late opening on account of it all and sorry 'bout the warm beer, but he'd just started up the cooler a couple of hours ago.

And so, on a flawless October night, when Eric Nowjack took me to the best restaurant in town and stumbled through a speech that I do not remember, handed me a box with a pipe cleaner ring in it, then another with a sparkling diamond, my head filled with fragrant love mist and I floated off my chair.

I have never cared much about jewelry, but that ring was the most divine thing I had ever seen. When we stepped into the night and passed another group of diners on their way into the Baricelli Inn, I stopped them.

"Look, look! Look at this ring! He asked me to marry him and I said yes!"

They smiled and laughed and congratulated us. After all, some of our good karma had splashed on them as well.

That's the easy part. The real test is, will you still be doing it with the lights on after 15 years?

Over the Threshold

Our house is the last one on a dead-end street—not a fancy pants cul-de-sac, mind you—a dead end. The street just stops, presumably to keep future access open to the large plot of undeveloped land next to us. The seclusion of the house was one of the reasons we purchased it. Our 1967 three-bedroom, split level ranch (complete with a "mother-in-law's suite" that is adjacent to the family room and consists of a eight-by-ten room with an impossibly small closet and a bathroom that would supposedly service the resident mother-in-law as well as any persons milling about the family room—a bad plan from the get-go) does not include a basement, (which was my husband's sole require-ment for a new home when we were house shopping), but instead features a utility room that is directly opposite the mother-in-law's/family room bathroom.

When we moved in, some parts of the house had been updated in the 1980s and included puffy mauve valences around the windows and those attractive wallpaper accent borders galloping around the top edges of the walls (soft non-threatening lions and teddy bears in one bedroom, a perpetual garland of some sort of flower that does not occur in nature in another). Loads of the original décor, however, still remained. The original brown and orange stripe motif still adorned one bathroom, mottled green glass sidelights graced either side of the front door and swinging saloon-style doors heralded the entrance to the kitchen. A series of decorative spiral spindles ranging from six to eight feet in length went between the vaulted ceiling of the living room and the half-walls that separated it from the entrance foyer.

We're talking mustard mosaic tile, oatmeal linoleum, and acres of wood paneling–all very BradyBunchesque with a side order of Huxtability (think the mid-80s Cosby Show). Thus was set the stage of our lives.

Over the years, we've done the usual home improvements: kitchen and bath updates, new furniture and a new front door. All of it contributes to a décor that's an Erin explosion. To start with, I paint every wall a different color, the staircase is blue, the kitchen is green, and the family room is red. The colors are a perfect backdrop to the menagerie of demons, imps and beastly onlookers that populate the house along with us regular humans.

African, Asian and Tiki masks glare from all points, while Buddhas gaze from coffee tables and curio shelves. A rotund clown, at once malevolent and bewildered, smiles at guests as they step through the front foyer. A vintage magic reproduction poster, "Dreamland" with Chevalier Earnest Thorn, is the focus of the living room, with its impish demons delighting over a golden cauldron from whence blue-green mist spills. A sinister horned man in a cape hovers over the magician Thorn as he contemplates it all, including a floating woman who stares longingly at him.

I prefer to keep the devil where I can see him.

I have a devil mask on one wall and another devil head on a stick that leans in a corner next to the front door. I wave it at selected incoming. For instance, I do a silly dance with the devil stick and holler something akin to, "goobladoobla ROWR!" just before dropping a KitKat into a costumed kid's sac on Halloween. The most fantastical of our resident devils appears above our mantle in a reproduction of "A Toast of Respect for Magical Prowess," in which magician Harry Kellar intertwines his arm around that of the most evil and luscious depiction of a demon I've ever come across. Unlike the smirking devil mask and stick, Kellar's devil is built for sin, androgynous in the most stunning way. The lines between his masculinity and femininity are hard drawn. His dark, angular and whiskered face grins out from beneath an elaborate hat that matches his voluminous gown, a red and black affair worthy of Scarlett and her transformed drapery. Mephistopheles' expression is one of irresistible inclusion as he meets Kellar's unwavering stare. Each is toasting with a large goblet of amber liqueur.

The myriad devils, imps and demons throughout the house are my resident nemeses. Often when I am en route from the bedroom to the laundry room, I will drop the basket of soiled clothing and grab the devil stick or step up upon the raised hearth and bore my eyes into Kellar's Mephistopheles.

"Quit with the eyeballing you son of a bitch," I will say to him and thereby vanquish any evil forces that might be at work against me and mine. The devils do not respond, but somewhere my brother smirks or nods or maybe sighs wistfully. Devils breaking through the walls were the prime terror hallucination of his delirium tremens, which, at least for me, has put an indelible question mark next to his lifelong and fervent assertions of atheism. Lord knows he claimed not to believe in God, but he sure as hell believed in the Devil. Suicide being what it is, I don't know if John finally succumbed to his devils or just escaped them. Hence I keep a bevy of devils around here as a reminder of my brother and his struggle. Unlike John, I always get the last word with all of my devils.

No worries, John, I've got these bastards covered for you. I won't let them out of my sight. Promise.

My husband's manifestation around our home is more cryptic. Once I found a shoe with a stalwart clamp on the toe atop the dryer. Was it a repair or a neo fly swatter? Only his hairdresser knows for sure. Another time he hauled our picnic table into the garage, upended it and strapped it to the wall. I didn't even try to figure that out, just took a photo by way of documentation and moved on.

There was the day that he stepped into the kitchen and announced, "I'm in recession mode," and plopped a four-liter bottle of Carlo Rossi "Reserve" Cabernet Sauvignon on the table.

I considered the massive jug. "It changes our whole house," I said.

"Gotta downgrade," he said, "the Depression's coming." This was during the financial slide of 2008.

He took great interest in determining the value of the Carlo Rossi. For that first jug, every time he "decanted" a glass, he'd mark the bottle.

"Looks like we'll get our mandatory 20 hits ... um, I mean pours," he said as he noted "pour" seventeen. He wanted to ensure that the $11 he spent for the Carlo Rossi was a better value than five 750 ml bottles of $3.29 Matthew Fox, which he theretofore purchased "exclusively" at the discount grocery.

He dutifully marked the next few jugs of Rossi with scores in the interest of "portion control" and concern that the sheer volume of the Carlo Rossi bottle would encourage excessive consumption. There were other marks on the labels, dates perhaps. I wasn't sure. My dearly beloved's writing does not look like writing at all, but instead like the tracks left by an itty-bitty Carlo Rossi inebriated chicken that had just stepped in ink.

The empty wine jugs posed a whole new challenge to our marriage.

As it is on earth, every Carlo Rossi jug doth come to an end. Thou art left with a glass bottle that houses approximately one gallon. Is this a thing of value? It is if I deem it to be, but it is not necessarily a thing of value if my husband deems it to be. Hence, when I first saw two such empty jugs in the "stupid room" (formerly the mother-in-law's suite, eventually renamed when it filled with things that were not necessarily stupid, but were in danger of becoming stupid for any number of reasons and saved because they had not yet breached the last Stupid Thing threshold), they did not strike me as inherently valuable, but more likely to become one of the things that I do not need that is obstructing access to one of the things I do need, and therefore the empty jugs were infuriating (although at the time, they were not obstructing anything) and in danger of becoming full-blown stupid things.

I am not an unfair person. I am every bit as infuriated by my own troubles with the previously mentioned container disease, which is not limited to empty margarine tubs, but also includes take-out food boxes that are "too good to throw away," darling little sushi to-go trays, inscrutable plastic cases that may have held sewing kits or travel-size versions of children's game or some other item that has long ago disappeared, and bags (your decorative gift category, your better shopping variety [read: with handles], and any sort composed of fabric). Many of these hideous container disease misfits are occupying space in the stupid room, where they take up too much space and irritate the hell out of me until I eventually give up and throw them all away the day before I need one of them. A gallon glass jug? The only thing I could ever imagine filling one with was pennies.

(Self, you have to admit, it would make a good penny jar. Not that you need a penny jar, or any jar that is suitable for housing a large volume of small items such as buttons or marbles or—heaven help us—$200 worth of Jelly Bellies)

I bit my tongue and decided not to say anything about the jugs until the numbers multiplied.

Cut to an otherwise picture perfect summer afternoon. My husband was returning yet again from the discount grocery (which, if the reader hasn't yet surmised, enjoys our patronage several times a week as we forget something—often the item that instigated the trip—nearly every time we go). I unpacked the bags as he unloaded the car.

I was inspecting an off-brand cereal he had purchased

called Sally's Sweet Puffs, which were designated on the package as being "Delicious, Nutritious and Satisfying!" A spoonful of Sally's Sweet Puffs was also prominently displayed. I was musing over this, thinking the puffs looked like tiny shaved vaginas when I heard my splendid king bark, "SHIT" from the drive.

I stepped out the front door, still holding the box of tiny shaved vagina cereal. My husband was standing over a gallon of milk that he presumably had just dropped. It had landed upright, with enough force to pop off the lid and blast out a couple of cups of the milk. Other than a broken lid, no other damage was done. The milk left in the plastic jug was completely potable.

"This one's all yours, hon," I said and sucked back into the house.

Up until that moment, I never thought I'd be smiling in satisfaction and pride at a glass gallon wine jug full of milk in the refrigerator, but as they say, every day is a winding road.

Avant-garde shoe flyswatters, tiny shaved vagina cereal and wine jugs full of milk notwithstanding, my husband is most regularly and simply evidenced in our household by the hallowed newspaper.

If the entire paper is hallowed to him, the sports page is sacrosanct. He does not simply read the sports page, he assimilates it. He studies every high school score, newswatch bit, and sidebar. Once when the print on the MLB stats column was smudged beyond readability, he spent an hour online rounding up the numbers. He files all the resulting information in his miserable brain, from whence it occasionally spills and makes him look like the household quirk genius.

"Al Sobotka?" I'll ask when the name spews from ESPN. "Who's Al Sobotka?"

"That's Detroit's octopus-swinging Zamboni guy."

"Huh?"

Although I am in no way entitled to feel this way, the whole sports thing irritates me. I have no idea why. Hence, I wait and watch for ways to poke at my dearly beloved's sports addiction.

Suppose for instance that my eyes flutter open on a Sunday morning only to spy my dearly beloved still slumbering peacefully beside me.

Which Erin am I at this moment? The soft wife might prevail and in that case, I'll nuzzle against my splendid king and relish in our holy union, hoping that his arms coil sleepily around me, and they usually do. But if I am possessed with the Other Erin, a different scenario altogether ensues.

Being as silent as possible, I turn onto my belly and slowly rotate myself, my toes squirming in search of the floor, then I slither out with a slow horizontal push and extract myself from our nuptial pleasure nest as quietly as possible. (Getting out of bed this theatrically is completely unnecessary. I only do it in order to impart a cartoon-like drama to the proceedings.) I creep out of the room and oh-so-gently-gently-gently shut the door behind me.

With shoulders hunched, a muffled giggle wheezing from my thin lips, and my hands malevolently wringing before me, I tiptoe downstairs and go directly into the utility room where the box of recyclable paper awaits. I dig into the pile and select a newspaper that's a few days old. From this I remove (oh evil delight!) the sports section. I extract the interior pages and bury the front page back in the box.

I carefully open the daisy-fresh, just-delivered Sunday sports section and remove the contents, keeping page one intact. Then, while occasionally peering over my shoulder like the Grinch checking for the unwelcome intrusion of Cindy Loo Who, I replace the new sports section interior with the old sports section interior, making sure to get all the folds and edges lined up with surgical precision. Then I shuffle the whole paper back together and casually toss it on the kitchen counter so it looks at once pristine and unassuming.

I tap my fingers on the Formica for about ninety seconds. Still no husband; no sounds of heavy footfalls descending the steps. I exhale my impatience with a sigh.

Coffee will wake him up! I retrieve the filter and slam the cabinet door. I fiddle loudly with the glass jar that houses our utility-grade joe and even embark on an emphatic coughing fit for good measure. It works. My splendid king lumbers down the stairs, snorting and scratching himself.

"Good morning!" I chirp.

"Mornin'."

Of course he has to read the goddamn paper in order, which puts the sports page much further down the road than I'm willing to wait, so in order to push him along I am forced to act like I want to read one of the front sections.

"Lemme see the headlines, hon."

That irritates him, although he says nothing and passes along section A.

My eyes dart between the paper before me and my husband, whose head and neck are maddeningly tortoise-like, sweeping slowly back and forth in perusal of the Metro section. I resist the urge to say something uncharacteristic such as, "So, what's shakin' with the Tribe?"

Finally he gets to the sports. He sips his coffee and takes in the Indians or Browns or Cavs headline. He opens to page two and finds the "Sunday Spin" exactly where it's supposed to be.

Things start getting dodgy about 30 seconds into page three.

His eyebrows collapse in confusion. He turns to the

next page, his lips in a one-sided curl. A turtle-head no more, his head snaps this way and that, then he turns back to page one, awash in consternation. After a few delicious moments of paper fluttering and muttering ("...what the... hmph...wait a minute...") that does not last nearly long enough, his eyes flatten into two suspicious slits, which he levels at Yours Truly.

Behold the purpose of life.

I've also been known to remove the Sports section entirely and hide it like a would-be Easter egg beneath the couch or stashed in the pots and pans cabinet.

It is important to note that evil pranks such as this are meaningless. No quarrel or disagreement precipitates them. Indeed, for the sports page switcheroo, the hiding trick, or the maneuver I'm about to describe to be effective, they must be a singular endeavor without anticipation.

You can manipulate the following scheme to work with almost any sporting event, but I like to use it on golf, which is a spectator sport without any spectacle. It's mystifying, really. A guy in bad clothing whacks a little ball. It's dumb. And if it's dumb in person, the golf telecast is the zenith of dumbness.

To illustrate my disapproval of televised golf, I sashay into the family room whilst a frenzied golf tournament broadcasts from our 20" CRT set (which is so low quality, it shadows all images it displays), nestle into the couch, and pretend to busy myself with a Sudoku puzzle. I wait for that incredibly irritating moment when the announcer's voice drops to the shhh-be-quiet-the-guy's-about-to-whack-the-ball tone (and is it just me or do all the golf announcers have annoying British accents?), which is my signal go into stealth mode. Just like that scene in *Jaws* when Quint's fishing line goes tick-tick-tick and he carefully buckles himself into the chair, I set down my *Super Fun Sudoku On the Go!* book and inch my hand over the couch towards the clicker.

As the camera follows the golf ball's path across a flawless blue sky where it has no scale or reference, but for some reason garners the acute concentration of viewers such as my husband, I wait with the remote clandestinely pointed at the box. When the parabolic trajectory of flight is just about to conclude on the green and thereby finally give the entire movement meaning, I give the channel return button a single click and it's goodbye British accent guy and sailing ball, hello QVC and the Victor Costa Occasion Beads & Sequins Floral Sweater (shown in seafoam) for the unbelievably low price of just $27.50.

Thusly, our marriage endures.

The Music of America

For the Goat and me, the road to "I do" took two years to travel. It spanned between Lakewood, Ohio (a suburb of Cleveland) and Austintown, Ohio (a suburb of Youngstown), and was exactly 82 miles long, for that was the distance between the dilapidated carport behind my brownstone apartment and the one-car garage adjacent to his modest ranch home. Every weekend, I either traveled to Nowjack's place or he came to mine. Hence, we became all too familiar with the stretch of the James W. Shocknessy Turnpike between exits 10 and 15 (which have since been renumbered to 161 and 218, respectively, in order to ostensibly "keep consistent with the federal standard for numbering interchanges on interstate highway systems," but really because the Ohio Turnpike Commission (ahem) miscalucated back in the 1950s when they said that tolling would end when the road was paid off and instead kept collecting tolls that had to be spent one way or another and thereby resulted in the addition of so many interchanges [3A, 3B, 7A, 7B, etc.] that the old number system became downright silly and confusing and they had to do something so they changed the exit names to correspond with the mile markers).

Our dating montage was a love story woven around the Rust Belt in the most organic sense. We ate out at places with Naugahyde covered seats and gingham tablecloths. The steak platter at Baratko's was $9.99.

"Blue cheese dressing and another whiskey sour when you have a chance, please."

There was the Riverwood Bar and the Kenilworth Bar and Bill's place, which Nowjack called "The Cheapest Bar in the World." True enough, the walls were covered with inarguable evidence that finding a better bargain on booze in the Mahoning Valley would be a very tall order indeed. Each hand-painted sign was more enthusiastic than the last.

All 12-ounce Domestic Draft: 75¢

Dewars $1.50!

STOLI 99¢!!

KESSLER 50¢!!!

Nowjack would sit at the bar, eyeing the game from the silent television while I sashayed over to the jukebox and tapped the glass cover, smoke curling from my Marlboro Light as I pursed my lips and considered the choices: three for a quarter and let's tap A04 for "I'm No Angel", by Greg Allman, B13 for Bowie's "Blue Jean", and C09 for

the Stones' "Little T&A." Such was a perfect accompani-
ment for me to perform on a small scale, dancing back to
my seat at the bar, and depending on the rhythm of the
song, shimmying or swaying on the stool. I punctuated all
of it with come-hither glances at my strapping beau.

Breakfast was eggs and bagels at John's Diner (my
side of town) or hash browns and "chopped steak" at
Luciano's (his side of town).

When we weren't riding that dazzling whirlwind, I
seduced him in either of our tiny kitchens with my culinary
charms. Add a packet of Mrs. Grass's onion soup mix to a
carton of sour cream and *Voila!* one pound of chip dip was
at my command.

"You made this?" Nowjack mused with wonderment
as he shoveled one Ruffleful after another into his mouth.

"Sure," I said, oozing savvy.

"Get out," he said, marveling over yet another loaded
chip.

Eric Nowjack went gaga over my pot roast (also
concocted with a packet of Mrs. Grass, but being complex
enough to require the obligatory can of Campbell's
condensed cream of mushroom soup); and salivated over
my spaghetti, which was borne of a jar of Prego, a half-
pound of browned ground meat, and a healthy shake of
Lawry's Seasoned Salt. He thought my toasted cheese was
a divine delivery worthy of a thousand loaves of Wonder

bread. Viva Velveeta, Viva middle America.

Ironically, when my domestic endeavors were the least successful, Nowjack's courtship efforts waxed most successful. An overzealous application of pepper to a pot of potato soup rendered it inedible, but Nowjack ate it just the same.

"You can't eat that slop," I said. "It's pure pepper!"

"So what's a little pepper?" he said, choking down a mouthful. "It's fine." That he ate the entire bucket despite his general-indifference-bordering-on-aversion to pepper was no small testimony to his character. Who needs shining armor with qualifications like that?

Nights "in" meant "Star Trek: The Next Generation" and giant slices of Wedgewood pizza ("the highest quality pizza in the Austintown area") or Lakewood's pride, Master Pizza (now defunct).

"Make it so, Number One."

One night he announced he would be making a pizza for me. I gazed up at him with starry eyes and squealed, "Homemade pizza?"

He proceeded to transform a packet of pizza crust mix, a half jar of sauce, some dehydrated onions, and generous shake of frozen shredded mozzarella cheese into a salted piece of cardboard.

"It's wonderful," I said dreamily.

Such were our sugary sweet weekends, at least until

Sunday morning rolled around.

Weather permitting, on Sundays Eric Nowjack would revert into his alter-ego of "Old Timer" and leave my nubile charms in order to join his cohorts (Eddie the Lover, Woody, Plugger, Hiroshima, BooBoo, Coffee Matt, Poops, Sparky, KeyMan, The Nick, Fish, Harpo, and Ye-Haw Bobby) to lope along the links. Despite the fact that he had been doing this since high school and was wholly entitled to do it, the all-male non-Erin Sunday excursions infuriated me. There was no justice in the world if a girl of my prowess and curvature got left on the bench, passed over for someone named Poops. It was demeaning.

I hid my aggravation with varying degrees of success, spending Sunday afternoons pining for him, curled up like a dejected puppy in my rattan Papasan chair. When he finally got home in the evening, I'd call and drown him with my cloying proclamations of love. Half the time, I'd be blubbering in my beer with the television on in the background.

"But I mm-mm-mm-miss you," I'd lament as Angela Lansbury's Jessica Fletcher snooped around trying to figure out just who in the heck would want to murder the husband of her temporary typist on "Murder, She Wrote".

"I know, Irish," he'd say while sipping a can of Pabst.

Then one day during our predictable Sunday night

boyfriend/girlfriend conversation, I heard some sort of music floating in the background.

I cocked my head in curiosity and asked, "Whatcha listening to, baby?"

"That?" said my prospective groom. "That's your *Music of America*, Irish."

In 1976, Ron Popeil's flagship company "Ronco" took a ride on the wave of Bicentennial patriotism that was sweeping the country and introduced *The Music of America*. The LP featured "Famous Memories–40–Favorite Songs; a commemorative bi-centennial recording" as performed by The Richmond Strings with the Mike Sammes Singers and available only through a special television offer for the unbelievably low price of just $7.99 (plus shipping and handling).

The contingent of readers who remember LP's are likely thinking that $7.99 was quite a bargain for a set of records large enough to accommodate 40 songs since standard LP's usually had about 10 or 12 songs on each record–enough to fill about 45 minutes. *The Music of America* was, perhaps surprisingly, only one record. Each of the 41 songs was condensed and truncated down to approximately one minute—an aural version of the *Reader's Digest* condensed book, if you will. (The discrepancy between the 40 songs denoted on the cover and the 41 listed on the back can be attributed to the fact that "America, The Beautiful" appears twice on the compilation: as an opening [Overture] and closing [Reprise], perhaps in a subtle nod to the assertion "from sea to shining sea!")

The album is organized into ten themed medleys, each one a short montage made up of excerpts from four or five songs. "The Civil War," for instance, begins with a sweeping sample of *Shenandoah*, segues into *When Johnny comes Marching Home*, then *Dixie*, then *Battle Hymn of the Republic*; whereas "The World Wars" features *Over There*, *Yankee Doodle Dandy* and *The Halls of Montezuma*.

The Music of America includes heartwarming cultural interludes as well. "The Railroad (Tribute To The Swing Era)" chug-a-lugs along with *Chattanooga Choo Choo*, *Take The 'A' Train* and *The Atchison, Topeka & The Santa Fe*; while "Stateside & Hollywood" takes a bustling tour of America by way of *California Here I Come*, *Deep in the Heart of Texas*, *Carolina In The Morning*, *Meet Me In St. Louis Louis*, and *Sidewalks Of New York*.

Every Single Word On The Song Listing Side Of The Album Jacket Is Capitalized And Printed In A Highly Stylistic Cursive Font.

A fellow writer once told me that writing about music is like dancing about architecture. You can try it, but you will fail. Even though she was referring to the foibles of one who tries to deliver a Rachmaninoff piano concerto by describing it with words, the same is true of *The Music of America*. You have to hear it to believe it, so I won't try to describe the music itself. All I can offer is this: imagine Lawrence Welk's "Musical Family" trying to be even more affable, conservative and non-controversial and you will approximate the effort of the Mike Sammes Singers on *The Music of America*. With the accompanying Richmond Strings, this group manages to dress a song like "Oh Susannah" in so much wholesome calico that Roy Roger's version of the same ditty looks like a streetwalker in fishnets and stilettos when compared to it. Even the instrumental version of "Beautiful Dreamer" takes the whitewashed American delusion to previously unimagined dimensions.

If it wasn't bad enough to relinquish my virile suitor to the likes of Coffee Matt and Ye-haw Bobby during the day, now I was losing him to "Old Man River" on Sunday nights.

"You're talking your American classics, Irish."

I would not have embraced *The Music of America* under any conditions, but because the record was part of his Sunday and I wasn't, I developed a vehement distaste for it. I was nearly jealous of it, just like his golf bag, but you can't really attack a record—unless you actually attack a record.

I am not proud to admit that I maliciously scratched *The Music of America*, but I did. I do not recall the specifics surrounding the event, but I'm pretty sure it was a repetitive clawlike vandalism accompanied by proclamations such as "This is SHIT!" However it played out, my efforts forever silenced Nowjack's copy of *The Music of America*, which would surely have this tale ending on a bitter note.

As time tumbled ineluctably forward, however, the phenomenon of the computer and the Internet and the unsinkable human proclivity for garage sales delivered unto us (of course) eBay.

"You oughtta see if you can find *The Music of America* on there," I said to my splendid king one day after years of marriage had mellowed my green-eyed tendencies to all but a silly and embarrassing memory.

About two weeks later, a copy of *The Music of America*, still in it's shrink-wrapped plastic, arrived on our doorstep. The pristine record was inside as expected, and (as promised on the cover) the contents included a "Special Bonus:" copies of the Constitution, The Declaration of Independence and the Bill of Rights (reproduced on beautiful high-quality "antique" parchment paper).

"These aren't in my original," said my dearly beloved with reverence as he pulled the yellowed copies from the sleeve. He squinted at the print, which was too tiny to read. "Now these are your real American documents," he said.

We dusted off the turntable, mounted the vinyl and powered her up. "America the Beautiful" spilled from the speakers.

The Goat shone like a beacon as "Swing Low Sweet Chariot" played, sang along heartily to "Sixteen Tons", and puffed with pride over "Home on the Range".

"This was back when America was America, not what we've got today," he said. "Where else can you get a collection like this in one place?"

"This," I said, pointing two thumbs behind me from whence the Mike Sammes Singers crooned, "is not a collection. You want to see a collection? I'll show you a collection." I bounded up the stairs and retrieved my DVD box set of Roger Corman classics. "Now this," I said, "is a collection. They even call it a collection right on the box: *The Roger Corman Collection*. See?" I held it up for his inspection. "This is brilliant," I said, eyeing the box. "You're talking *Bloody Mama*, *The Man with the X-Ray Eyes* and *GAS-S-S-S*. 'Crazed hooligans, red-hot babes,' and debauchery,' this set has it all. Its even got Shelley Winters! You got any Shelley Winters on your *Music of America*?"

"No, but I've got the Constitution," he said righteously, and started singing along to "The Streets of Laredo".

"As I walked out in the streets of Laredo," he warbled as our daughter came into the kitchen, "As I walked out in Laredo one day ..."

Our baby dumplin' looked at him and wrinkled her nose.

I bent down and put my hands on either of her shoulders. "I'm sorry, kid." I said. "I knew all about this and I still married him. I still married him!" I held her gaze for another pendulous moment, then let the cadence of my voice collapse with defeat. "I'm so so so sorry, kid."

She blinked at me once or twice and said, "It's okay, Mom," and turned on the small kitchen boom box. Bubble gum heartthrob Aaron Carter rang out, pitting a righteous fight against "The Halls of Montezuma" coming from the living room. I stood there marveling over this unlikely match in which the figurative contenders were an 18-year-old battling premature ejaculation and an 80-year-old with an empty bottle of Viagra. It was as terrible a thing as I'd ever witnessed.

Fortunately, it didn't last long. When "The Entertainer" lilted from the living room, Jessie's ears pricked. She quickly turned off her stereo to listen more closely.

"Ice cream truck!" she blurted. After all, it was the same ditty that heralded the arrival of the Capt. Kool's traveling dairy emporium.

"No honey," I said. "That's not the ice cream truck.

This is still Dad's music." Disappointment washed over her and she slunk back outside to her sidewalk chalk.

"I hope you're happy," I said to the Goat, "disappointing a little kid like that," as if she didn't get disappointed almost every time Capt. Kool rolled down our street and her hopeful look was squelched with "It's only an hour before dinner. NO."

Hence the Goat was undaunted by my thin ruse. He was, in fact, very happy as he floated through the house along with Mike Sammes and the gang. He played the record again and again to extend the euphoria. I even caught myself bouncing along to "The Atchison, Topeka & The Santa Fe", which is when the music came to a sad sslllloooowwwww eeeeennnnnnd.

It took about four minutes to determine the 25-year-old turntable had malfunctioned.

"It croaked," I said obviously enough, but inside I felt bad for the Goat. Purchasing *The Music of America* was the first time I'd ever seen him go out of his way to buy himself any sort of music. Ever. I had no idea what to do about the problem of the defunct turntable, so as my darling groom went in search of the toolbox, I went to busy myself with the seemingly ever-present task of potato peeling.

A half-hour later he came into the kitchen with the remnants of a broken black rubber band dangling from his thick fingers.

"The belt disintegrated," he said, holding it up for my inspection.

"Looks that way," I responded. "Sorry about that, Hon." He puzzled over it, then ambled away wordlessly. I turned back to the cutting board and waiting spuds.

A person does not expect there to be a connection between the half-pound "economy" bag of rubber bands that a person paid 50 cents for at the discount grocery from the oddlots bin and The Richmond Strings with The Mike Sammes Singers and their stirring rendition of "The Star Spangled Banner", but that's what makes life beautiful.

The Goat retrieved said bag of rubber bands and returned to the disassembled turntable. After a few trials, he found a large rubber band that approximated the duty of the ruined belt. The player's operation recommenced and the rubber band held out long enough for Nowjack to commit all of *The Music of America* to a cassette tape, the quality of which is dodgy at best. A buzz/hum waxes and wanes for the entire duration, which is longer than intended due to a discrepancy with the rubber band/belt repair and the nuances of the turntable's pitch adjustment. The Goat was undeterred by any of this. He inserted the tape into his the dash of his Mercury Sable, where he played it as he drove over hill and dale, his left foot tapping gently upon the floor and his right hand keeping time upon knee.

So it remained until the year of Our Lord, 2010.

Tending the Grounds

Our neighborhood is located in an outer-ring suburb of Cleveland in the midsection of Northeast Ohio. I call the area the Cleveland Alps due to its elevation, which also designates our environs as the secondary snowbelt. Although we supposedly do not get as much snow as the primary snow belt (the northernmost portion of the state on the shores of Lake Erie that is geographically prone to the combination of an icy westerly wind [the Jet Stream] that picks up moisture from the open waters of the lake before it freezes over in the winter, transforms said newly acquired moisture into snow and deposits it on the nearest available landfall), we get one hell of a lot of snow.

And when the frigid skies open above us and blanket our tiny corner of the earth in a thick layer of white, my husband dutifully muscles the pull cord of the Toro snow blower and clears the drive. This is a source of great comfort to me. There were a handful of years in my adolescence during which my father waded through a lackadaisical period and shoveling the drive was not a priority. When it would snow heavily and the municipal snowplow would aggravate the situation at the very end of the drive where the snow removed from the street would add to Mother Nature's accumulation, getting vehicles in or out was a dodgy proposition at best. My brother drove a 1965 baby blue Mustang at the time. He would try to defy the bulge of snow at the end of the drive by accelerating into it. As often as not, the Mustang would end up solidly stuck in the bank, precluding any trips that were of interest to me: a ride to the local ice skating rink, my Saturday morning acting class or the weekly grocery trip with Mom.

Hence, when my splendid king clears our drive from snow, I will sometimes burrow my terrible self betwixt the pillowy leather cushions of the couch by the front window and peer out with my Eringator eyes as he moves about the yard in his personal blizzard, a snow-suited Pigpen encased in a cloud of icy white instead of dust and dirt.

But as comforting as it is, the most notable outcome of these proceedings is not a navigable driveway. When my husband is righteously finished with the task at hand, he stands proud, one hand on hip, the other upon the Toro's handle—a true master of his domain. Not only is the drive and apron snow-free, but our section of the sidewalk, upon which feet rarely tread even in the fairest of weather, is a neat 100-foot tunnel in the snow. Why do I draw attention to this portion of his efforts? Because ours is the last segment of sidewalk on our dead-end street and is invariably the only one that is cleared. This has not deterred his vigilance since we took up residence on the property in 1992.

There is a concrete pad bordered by the street, our sidewalk and our property line that the city installed to facilitate large vehicle turn-around in lieu of a cul-de-sac. Whenever I am obliged to park on the auxiliary pad in the winter, I draw inordinate attention to the fact that I'm walking on the cleared sidewalk (although I could just as easily walk in the street).

"No problems here. My path is sure clear!" I trumpet in order to subtly acknowledge my appreciation of his efforts. Even so, I don't see our finite sidewalk tunnel as a simple husbandly quirk. For Eric Nowjack, this is not just snow removal, it's performance art.

The fairer months harbor different domestic battles.

On a clear spring morning when my daughter was about four months old, I was at the task of changing her. After taking care of business, I took the opportunity to tickle and coo and giggle as she gazed up at me from the top of the baby cabinet. A near perfect scene until a black ant descended upon it, scurrying across my darling infant daughter's peach colored belly.

"Honey," I said that evening to my dearly beloved, "it's time to call an exterminator."

After the initial sales call, our account was assigned to Bill, which is how he introduced himself both in person and per the embroidered patch on his rough cotton work shirt. Bill became one in the parade of men with shirts with name patches and vans with tools that have visited our home over the years, each of which (with a few exceptions) endeared themselves to me in one way or another.

There was Al the plumber: "Don't put anything in your toilet that wasn't in your mouth first," and Ray the diaper man: "You see this?" he'd say of my plastic bag of soiled diapers during his weekly drop. "These smell GOOD compared to what I'm picking up at my NEXT stop." Sufficient cajoling would reveal that Ray's next stop was a home for the elderly.

There was the foreman of the roofing crew with his ragtag men who changed daily depending on their parole status. They descended upon my house in the middle of a hot, humid and merciless July. The work itself was horrible. The guys hammered away on the roof, sweating and swearing and slapping at wasps.

"What's the problem, girls?" the foreman would shout from the ground as he chewed a doughnut. "Now you girls are afraid of a couple of bugs?"

But Bill the exterminator had tag lines that Madison Avenue couldn't have come up with. On his first trip out, he stood in my utility room, hands on hips and said with a practiced delivery, "Ma'am, you and I use Interstate 77 to travel from here to there. But carpenter ants?" he paused with great import as he pointed a thumb at the grid of plumbing on the wall behind him. "They use your water pipes." He returned his hand to his hip, grinned and nodded knowingly.

About two days after his initial treatment, I was lying in bed when I felt a tickle on my back. Then another. There was black ants running all over me.

"Bill," I said on the phone, "I've got some uninvited visitors in the bed." It seemed I'd barely hung up the phone before he was at my door.

"Told the boss one of my Missus had an emergency," he said and went on to explain that the ants were "freaking out" due to the extremely dry conditions and the recent pesticide application. "They're desperate," he said. "But don't worry, I've got it under control."

Bill came once a month. At the conclusion of his visit, we'd sit at the kitchen table where he'd explain to me what he did and then I had to sign a paper.

"'Fraid to tell you that I won't be here next month, but don't worry. Dave'll take real good care of you."

"You're not leaving the company, are you, Bill?" I asked.

"No, no," he said affably. "Nothing like that. Going on vacation. Going to see my kids." He explained that they lived in California. "A-course, that means I'll be running into the Wicked Witch of the West," he added, indicating his ex-wife.

Perhaps she cast a spell upon Bill, because I did not see him again after that. We stepped through the remaining months of the contract with Dave, who was every bit as efficacious as Bill, but lacked that certain verve.

After that, the Goat found an industrial supply house that carried the same pesticides the professionals used, so that became another of his DIY tasks.

There are other creatures that many would not consider to be pests that the Goat views a bit differently. In his realm, there are simple pests, and there are more formidable nemeses.

Due to the healthy population of oaks in our neighborhood, the resident squirrels are not skinny little black squirrels, but big fat brown squirrels. When I say fat, I mean FAT. The squirrels here are so fat, I call them turkey squirrels.

When we moved into this house, we erected a bird feeder, which the turkey squirrels promptly took over in a backyard occupation of sorts. As if the annual proliferation of acorns was not enough, they had to go and eat all the birdseed as well. This irritated my husband to no end. So I purchased a "squirrel-proof" bird feeder for him one Christmas, the feeding perch for which is on a cantilever mechanism. If too much weight is on the perch, it closes the feeding trough.

I have names for some of the squirrels, one of which I call Evil Canevil. He got his name one day as I was gazing out the window and spied a squirrel running across a thin maple branch. This was no regular turkey squirrel, this was a category 5 turkey squirrel, as round in the middle as my own fleshy thigh.

So he's hauling ass across the branch, which is swaying and dipping like all get out and that situation is getting worse the farther he gets away from the trunk. But this squirrel doesn't miss one beat. He keeps going. Then he jumps.

His terrible squirrel body hurls spread-eagle through the air and goes about eight feet before landing on the end of another thin branch of another tree, which REALLY dips and sways.

By then, I was captivated by the spectacle. "Whoa!" I blurted in amazement. From then on I called him Evil Canevil because (1) he's evil, (2) he can and (3) he's a daredevil just like his namesake of a different spelling.

The next sentence is as predictable as a stain in a pair of white underwear: It took Evil Canevil and the turkey squirrel contingent about seventeen seconds to defeat the squirrel-proof bird feeder. They found a way to support their weight on the adjacent tree and hold open the perch.

So my husband moved the feeder. Then they supported their weight from the chain from which the feeder hung. So my husband replaced it with a thin wire they could not negotiate.

Evil Canevil was however, persistent. He'd get on top of the feeder by jumping from the adjacent tree. The metal was slick and watching him land was always funny, but particularly funny if it was wet and his horrible little feet frantically scratched as he'd lose his grip and fall. He had his share of victories as well. When he did get a good footing, he'd stay up there picking out the goods from the feeding perch until the bin was empty or he was full/tired. He had to be very careful or the 'squirrel-proof' counter weight would engage and shut off supply.

"Smart One," another of the turkey squirrels, would stay on the ground eating what Evil Canevil dropped.

The Goat tried any number of techniques in order to discourage Evil Canevil and Smart One from feeding from the squirrel-proof bird feeder, including adding ingredients to the seeds that make them unappetizing to squirrels. He had half my kitchen out in the back yard, where he mixed and stirred like a seven-year-old with her first Easy Bake oven. His efforts paid off, but the Goat desired a more permanent solution.

"Something you don't need to maintain," he explained.

So he put a flange on top of the squirrel-proof bird feeder, which Evil Canevil appreciated as it gave him something from which to hang. This was not the outcome the Goat intended, so he put up a larger flange. Unfortunately, the new flange caused excessive wind resistance, making the feeder spin at approximately 1000 RPM in a good breeze, effectively disallowing any creature from using it. In order to remedy this side effect, the Goat added another horizontal tether from the feeder to the host tree in order to keep the squirrel-proof bird more-or-less stationary. This arrangement has been fairly successful.

The only birdseed available to peripheral feeders such as the turkey squirrels is what the birds drop on the ground. During spring and fall, however, Smart One and Evil have to contend with the Canadian goose. I call him "BadAss."

Unless there are nocturnal battles with ground hogs and raccoons of which I am unaware, no one messes around with BadAss except my husband, who hates BadAss—although he's not too happy with Smart and Evil either. The Goat thinks the only creatures that should partake of the birdseed (either in the feeder or on the ground) are birds. I have pointed out to the Goat that BadAss is a bird, but apparently there is a Goat-determined size limitation on Birds That Are Authorized To Feed At The Squirrel Proof Bird Feeder for which BadAss does not qualify.

Sometimes the Goat will chase after BadAss with a

stick. BadAss watches him approach and starts casually walking away. He picks up speed along with the Goat and eventually takes flight. The Goat has never caught BadAss, whom I think prolongs the chase as long as he can in order to amuse himself.

I felt bad for the Goat with all his perils, so I went and bought him some thistle and a new feeder. It took a few days, but the finches finally found it. They feed on it all day without interruptions from BadAss, the Smart One or Evil Canevil.

"Those finches sure like that thistle," says the Goat as he grins and watches their peaceful repast.

They certainly do like the thistle. If I thought the squirrels could pack on the pounds, the finches are the avian equivalent to Sumo wrestlers. They don't even look like birds anymore, but oversized feathered softballs with beaks, the little bastards.

But they are little and their mechanical pecking seems to make the Goat happy. When the Goat is happy, the wife of Goat is happy. If we're lucky, the teen daughter of Goat is also happy and the three of us are content to sit backwards on the couch that is in front of the front window and peer out at the fat finches and down our driveway and across the street and up at the sky and beyond the blue where the sun and moon and stars and the endless universe spill out forever.

Stepping Out

"You're slowing down," I'll say. "Why are you slowing down?"

There is no reason for me to ask this question. I have witnessed my husband slowing down for green lights for 19 years. But this battle, since it is playing out in the front seat of the car, is unique. Unlike disagreements over hearth and home, car wars do not dissipate. Conversely, they refresh. The fact that my husband slows down for a green light never surprises me but always stuns me. I am unable to permanently process this behavior.

"It's a green light," I'll say. "Green means GO, remember?"

"What you got here," he'll respond, "is a stale green light."

Therein lies an ultimate truth: two separate views of the universe, both clearly verifiable while being diametrically different. Half of the population would speed up because the green light, as they always do, will soon turn yellow. The other half slows down for the exact same reason. Whichever kind of person you are, you will marry the other kind. That is the irrevocable way of the world. The mythical anti-matter anti-world is not floating in some ulterior universe. It is alive and well and sitting right next to you in the front seat. The question is: can you handle it?

Marriage classes for Mormons and Catholics are meaningless. Same with matchmaker questionnaires for that lonely heart contingent that swells and deflates online. Want to put your heavy squeeze to a lifelong compatibility test? Drive from Detroit to Albuquerque. If you don't kill each other somewhere along the way, you pass. Go on and get hitched.

That is not to say that your significant other's road quirks won't drive you up a wall. Just watch me huff and fidget anytime my husband crawls toward a green light.

"Why don't you just pull over and die?" I'll say, arms crossed over my chest as we inch towards the intersection.

"What'd I tell you?" he'll say with righteous indignation as the light turns yellow and he slows from the dastardly speed of 4 MPH to a dead stop.

"Of course it turned yellow," I'll say. "Green lights always turn yellow. They don't do anything else. Turning yellow is a green light's sole eventuality."

"Stale green light," he'll say, ending the discussion until we have it again in six or seven months.

The stale green light business is just one function of his inherent inverse-speed behavior. If there is a reason to hurry, my husband slows down. Conversely, if we are under no time constraint, he speeds up. I believe the slow-down-when-we-really-need-to-hurry part of the equation is some deep-rooted control thing. When we're traveling 13 MPH down a 35 and the Goat is squinting up at the sky saying something inane such as, "Looks like it's trying to snow," when the movie starts in four minutes, the subliminal message he's trying to impart is: *There's no rush. I've got this all under control.* In order to reinforce that assertion, upon arriving at the multiplex, he will walk through the parking lot at a slower-than-usual rate, hitching up his pants and snapping his head to and fro, an exhibition of his superlative power of observation.

"Sure are packing them in today, huh?"

If, however, there is absolutely no reason to rush, the Goat attributes his speeding to some force beyond his control, gravity for instance.

"Is there a reason you're going 55 in a 35 when we have absolutely no place to be other than on the couch watching a "Star Trek" rerun?" I'll ask.

"We're on a hill," he'll say with a cadence and inflection that imply I must be half bonkers to suggest he has anything to do with the vehicle's speed. "I'm not even on the gas."

"So if an officer of the law stops you," I'll say, "is that what you're going to tell him? That you weren't even on the gas? That the earth's formation is responsible for your speed?"

"It's gravity" he'll say. "I'm coasting."

Me? I don't turn left.

"Why aren't you turning left?" my husband will ask.

"Because I don't like to turn left," I'll respond.

"Why don't you like turning left?" he'll say. "It's just turning left."

"Why turn left if you can turn right?" I'll pose.

"But how are we going to get home if you don't turn left?"

"By turning right," I'll say, ending the discussion until we have it again in six or seven months.

Car talk is also clothed pillow talk in motion.

"Don't those brown salt bin thingies look like giant road boobs?" I'll opine.

"Road boob," my dearly beloved will concede.

"What do you suppose the "REST RANT" is?" I'll say of a passing sign. "Maybe someplace where you can take a nap or blow off steam by yelling at a person in a booth?"

"Or a regular REST-AU-RANT sign that's missing the AU," my husband will offer.

My husband's regional colloquialisms often surface

during travel.

"Once we get to Beaumont," my husband will say, "you're talking thirty, maybe forty miles nort."

"Nort?" I'll respond.

"Nort," he repeats.

"Do not say 'nort.'"

"What?" my husband will innocently ask. "You asked where the exit was and I told you: thirty-some miles nort of Beaumont."

"It's norTHHH, not norT," I'll say. Nort sounds like a robot villain in a science fiction movie. Say 'north.'"

"Nort."

There was the time we were driving through pastoral Findlay, Ohio and a man to whom we later bequeathed the title "Red Raider" was sauntering past the quaint century buildings of Main Street, with their long Italianate windows and stone facades. Nothing unusual really, until you consider he was wearing a skin-tight red Lycra body suit, complete with cape and booties, the chest portion of which was scooped down nearly to his belly button.

Although I say he was sauntering, it was more like a moving performance. He would commence an exaggerated march, stop, victoriously punch his fists upward, twirl around, and so on. Not what you expect to see on a street festooned with red, white and blue swags hanging from vintage streetlights.

"Look to your right, hon," I said.

"Huh?"

"Just look to your right."

He finally spied the Red Raider as he swirled his cape around.

"Yup," said my husband appropriately enough. Some things defy comment.

Then there are the mundane exchanges in which I am obliged to say wifely things such as, "Why don't you take 480? You don't really want to take Brookpark, do you? All those lights? Brookpark will take forever!"

"I just steer the bus," would be my husband's flat and slightly disgusted response as he veers towards the highway sign. This is a man who picks his battles.

Over the years, I've kept track of my husband's singular terminology and have thereby compiled a glossary. It includes entries such as "Universal Repair," a method by which one repeatedly impacts an inoperable piece of equipment with either one's foot or a hammer.

I've seen the Goat subject tires, wooden steps and toilets to Universal Repair with varying degrees of success. Admittedly, his car door once responded favorably to this method.

"Kicked it and now the auto-lock key chain thing is working again."

Sadly, however, the execution of Universal Repair

on a four-foot ice column negatively impacted our front picture window one winter.

"Goddamnit anyway!"

Although Universal Repair is a seasoned entry in my Goat Glossary and surely worthy of this diversion, it pales in comparison to the phrases he applies to certain driving situations.

Running Interference: Term used to describe a fellow motorist who is driving far in excess of the posted speed limit. An "interference" vehicle secures an undetermined portion of the highway by diverting the attention of any law enforcement representative that may be standing by ahead.

I first heard this term after expressing dissatisfaction with the speed my husband was traveling on the Turnpike.

"Jesus Christ awmighty!" I screamed. He was going 80 MPH, a speed I engage without hesitation, but that of course, is different. "What's your goddamn hurry?"

"No hurry," he said. "We got this guy here." He was lazily wagging his cigarette at a passing car (while I gave up the sticks a year after our holy matrimony began, my dearly beloved smoked up until two pink lines indicated that a bundle of joy was on the way). "Guy's running interference."

"Running interference?" I said.

"Cop sees this guy coming down the pike at 90? What's that cop care what I'm doing?"

It took a moment for this to sink in.

"You're shitting me, right?" I said finally.

"What?" he said. "Guy's running interference."

"The guy could slow down. Or exit," I said. "Another cop could enter the highway between you and him."

My husband ignored me and continued. "And when you see your interference man stopped with a cop, you know you lost your safety net, but even then there's an added benefit. You got one less cop to worry about, at least for the time being."

"The cop who stopped the interference guy?" I said. "What are you talking about? You still have to pass him."

"Doesn't matter" said my husband with satisfaction. "That cop's *copupied*."

Copupied: lingual amalgam of cop and occupied; term used to describe a law enforcement representative who is assisting another motorist.

Once again, I offered my critique. "The cop's got a phone or radio or something, maybe some massive cop-computer system that he can use to talk to all cops from here to Shitkanistan!" I said and, once again, my dearly beloved ignored me.

"Copupied," he said.

But my favorite deluded-Goat phenomenon is only applicable during inclement weather.

Rainar: Lingual amalgam of rain and radar; phenomenon by which radar speed detection is nullified by falling precipitation.

"Way I figure is that the cop radar rays shoot out of the radar gun," said my husband. "Right?"

"Right," I said.

"But instead of hitting your car," he said, grinning conspiratorially and lowering his voice, "the cop rays hit the raindrops."

"Uh-huh," I said.

Marriage is many things, including a slow behavioral transference. For instance, I'd like to think myself above Universal Repair, but I am not.

Once while cleaning, I ran across a small wooden stool gifted to me by a relative with whom I had had a precipitous falling out, the result of which had my mother and I entangled in an emotionally fraught lawsuit for over two years.

Seeing the stool, I became so incensed over the whole

situation (in which we were still embroiled), that I took it out to the drive, smashed it to pieces with a hammer, kicked the debris across the lawn, then threw the hammer over my shoulder and went back inside.

Unbeknownst to me, the spectacle had drawn my neighbor's attention from the task of cleaning that day. She'd watched my Universal Repair of the stool from her bathroom window.

Her car pulled up beside me as I went for walk later that afternoon. "Have a problem this morning?" she asked.

"Nope," I said. "Just doing a little repair work," to which she nodded knowingly and said, "Yep," rolled up her window and went on her way.

So the assimilation is underway but not yet complete. Perhaps I'll say "nort" instead of "north" by the time we celebrate our Silver Anniversary. For now, I must admit that as I maneuver through my endless right turns on a rainy day, I fancy myself under my own invisible umbrella. After all, isn't rainar just another way to say universal copupation?

Shop Talk

The unfortunate admission that I occasionally shop at WalMart heralds from the same realm as the purchase of a whole ham or giant pork, wherein convenience and economics band together and tower above me, menacing and threatening until I succumb, and I always do. Frugality is hard-wired into my genetics. My distaste for WalMart's big box store mentality is significant. To reach the tipping point when I swallow it all whole is notable, attained only with a certain kind of list.

When the need for athletic socks and Windex and Reduced Fat Triscuits and Suave Water Rinsable Cold Cream (yes, I am one of the six remaining women in the world who still uses cold cream) converges with the need for blank CDs and a new hose spigot and Rain-X (arguably the most efficacious product on the market today) and a new drink shaker thingie (used primarily for the proper mixing of chocolate milk) that you need after melting the old one in the dishwasher and that you are not sure you will be able to replace, I am faced with a distinct prospect. I can do it the hard way and head to TJMaxx for the socks, the discount grocery for the crackers and Windex (and probably the cold cream, but they may not have it and in that case it would mean a trip to the dreaded Discount Drug Mart), the Sears Hardware for the Rain-X and spigot (the drink shaker is one of those items that you look for everywhere you shop), and OfficeMax for the CDs. Or I can just go to WalMart.

Grrrr!

A WalMart list is not only daunting in its sheer magnitude, but as indicated by the sampling above, it is also usually bisexual in nature. Hence, when I head to the land of the yellow smiley face, my splendid king will accompany me as often as not. Therefore, on a rainy spring day during the seventh year of our marriage, when the household list burgeoned beyond the confines of supermarket or discount grocery, we went off to feed the grotesque monster born from Sam Walton's quaint variety store in Newport, Arkansas.

We had split up in order to cover our respective territories. My splendid king went in search of the automotive aisle as I headed for the shores of health and beauty.

Therein I was, duly inspecting a box of deep cleaning pore strips that you wet and put on your nose and allow to dry into some sort of mysterious cosmetic cement then pull off in order to remove what has been residing in the tiny off in order to remove what has been residing in the tiny holes of your skin. As I was taking comfort in the fact that the eighteen-and-flawless chick on the box with the strips plastered on her nose and forehead (making them look like some sort of soft-core gas mask) looked every bit as unattractive as I do when I use them, my attention was called away.

"Attention shoppers," came a voice smooth as velvet from above, "we will be handing out free paring knives in Housewares in 20 minutes." I threw the pore strips into my cart and tried to ignore the announcement (a free paring knife?) by focusing on whether or not the scent of Suave Clarifying shampoo was pleasant enough for my refined tastes.

Next I was dithering over the gut-wrenching decision to buy or not to buy a plastic tumbler that I absolutely did not need (but only cost 99 cents–same as the shampoo). Made in China. Top rack dishwasher safe.

"There's just 15 minutes left, shoppers, before you can pick up your free surgical stainless steel paring knife in Housewares."

Surgical steel?

"And this high quality piece of cutlery comes with a lifetime guarantee," said the unseen voice as I dropped two of the tumblers into my cart.

Lifetime guarantee? Free?

Clearly an investigation was in order. I needed to enlist the formidable skills of my husband. After all, we were talking a Free Surgical Steel Lifetime Guaranteed piece of Cutlery here, not just some lousy knife. I found Nowjack in menswear staring with bewilderment at his reflection in a mirror. "Supplies are limited," purred the announcer as my splendid king tugged at the waistband of a pair of stiff jeans and pivoted one leg on the ball of his foot.

"Do these fit?" he asked me.

"Honey!" I barked with none of the sweetness the word implies. "You've got to get to Housewares," I said as the mellow voice extolled the virtues of Better Cutlery.

"Housewares? Why would I go to housewares?" he asked, doing a mini knee bend. "Do you think these fit?"

Realizing that there are no short cuts in life, I exhaled a huge demonstrative wife sigh. "This," I said while indicating the immediate space around my corporeal person," is my sphere of existence."

"You don't think they're too big, do you?" he said.

"I need only concern myself with the proceedings within said sphere," I said, undaunted. "If there is hunger within, I seek nourishment. If there are questions, I seek answers. If there is a need to improve the environment within my sphere, I seek a can of Glade Air Wick.

"That," I said, indicating the space around my husband with a flourish of waving fingers, "is your sphere of existence. In it, you are responsible for the proper fitting of new jeans, the responsible consumption of Budweiser and Durkee Potato sticks, and an acceptable amount of Irish Spring ablutions.

"Within the confines of said jeans," I continued, "I know not if you require," I scratched the air on either side of my head with two hooked fingers, indicating the placement of two quotation marks around what I was about to say, "a 'skosh' more room around your nether parts."

"Now then, if, for instance, I were to saunter over to the women's department and strap on a utility-grade 38C 24-Hour Cross Your Heart, I would have to worry about whether or not the associated garment tugged, drooped or pinched. Understand?" I indicated the space around me again. "My sphere of existence," and the space around my spouse, "your sphere of existence."

We blinked at each other in the wake of my speech.

"Furthermore," I added, taking advantage of my momentum, "I should think that after having walked the earth since the Paleozoic age, you should know whether or not an article of clothing is right for you." I paused yet again. "Over there," I said, jabbing a finger toward him. "In your sphere."

"Do these fit?" he said.

"That's right, shoppers," interrupted the announcer's voice, "in just five minutes, we'll be handing out a limited number of surgical stainless steel paring knives absolutely free. These top quality knives are guaranteed for life and—now pay attention shoppers—they never need sharpening."

"Yes," I said hurriedly. "They fit. They fit perfectly. Now hurry up and change and GET ME ONE OF THOSE PARING KNIVES!"

"Why don't you go?" he asked.

"Because of this," I said, waving my list of 65 absolutely annoying items (Pledge, duct tape, coffee filters) in his face.

"And there's no obligation," said the unseen voice.

"Yeah, right," said my husband, raising his eyes skyward.

"You Goat!" I bellowed as my hair transformed into a mass of writhing serpents. "Get to Housewares!"

He rolled his eyes and stomped off without a word.

After about a half hour, my dearly beloved had not reappeared. I pushed my tinfoil- and Ritz- laden cart towards the hills and valleys of wastebaskets and Pyrex, otherwise known as Housewares.

An amoeba-like throng of hair-sprayed housewives was tightly packed in front of the velvet voiced announcer, who turned out to be the very definition of smarmy. He had dirty fingernails, jet-black hair and a waxed pencil-thin mustache. A pencil-thin mustache for chrissake! He was standing before an assortment of severed Pepsi cans and tomatoes and tennis balls. The mountain of paring knives was piled behind him, as captive as his listeners for the duration as he recounted the myriad and compelling reasons to purchase a complete set of Japanese Miracle Blade Knives for the unbelievably low one-time-only introductory price of $39.95. It was clear no one was going to get a free paring knife until they had listened to everything–and I mean everything–that spilled from beneath that sharp black line of facial hair.

Eric towered above all the women in their oversized sherbet colored sweatshirts. He was imprisoned up front, getting squashed and shoved, patiently listening with a forced smile on his face.

And, although I was laughing so hard that tears squeezed from my eyes, inside I melted with dizzying, idiotic love for him.

The Nuptial Bed

Each night the blissful peace of slumber falls upon me and I become Sleeping Erin, one lofty cloud away from Sleeping Beauty or her fairy-tale cousin, that sensitive princess with the pea. Moonlight spills over Sleeping Erin as she lay in repose, loosely draped in silken bed linens and dappled in moonlight. Each breath is a tiny mortal tide, advancing and retreating from her lungs with orchestrated smoothness. Sleeping Erin's dreams are beauteous events, replete with colorful things floating weightlessly among cinnamon-scented clouds.

Yeah, right.

I don't just snore. I saw wood like a chainsaw, performing what is called "heroic" snoring, which the University of California's health science page defines as being loud enough to be heard more than two bedrooms away. Two bedrooms? I think they can hear me in Akron.

I inherited heroic snoring from my father, whose nightly snores would crescendo to a startling decibel level until finally, he would wake with a start and yell something like, "Holy Christ! That's 17 tons of salt!" all of which could be heard throughout the solidly built brick home of my childhood.

My own snoring is so vigorous that I often wake with a condition I have playfully dubbed "snore throat:" a gullet so raw from sawing wood that whenever I wake with it, I tell my delusional self that such a condition could not possibly be from snoring. To that end, I check the status of my tonsils throughout the day for signs of distress (such signs never appear and the severity of the snore throat predictably lessens over the course of the day proving with each passing minute that, yes, I do snore that violently).

The worst case of snore throat I ever had was after the birth of my daughter. I was in the hospital room after many hard hours of labor. My new baby was in the nursery so I could finally catch some sleep before I took her home and the daunting career of motherhood began in earnest. The nurse gave me a sleeping pill, to which I felt wholly entitled.

When I woke the next morning with the grand-daddy of snore throats, that I could barely swallow is not what disturbed me. The fact that I treated all those new moms and their little babies in the hospital to the rhythmic sound of a jackhammer all night? Now that bothered me. It's amazing they didn't converge on my room and lynch me.

When I am not snoring in the wee hours, I am engaging

in any number of other activities. I drink about 20 ounces of water during the night and therefore deposit 20 ounces of Erin-processed liquid into the Northeast Ohio Regional Sewer District's network. I read, go to the computer, peer out windows, practice yoga, saunter around the house, and of course, snack. (But really, when your standing naked before the unearthly glow of your freezer at three in the morning with a pint of Rocky Road in one hand and a spoon in the other, doesn't that preclude the relevance of everything else? Does it not embody the assertion: You Are Here?)

"You do more when you're asleep than most people do when they're awake," my husband says.

Sometimes I am awake for these activities and some-times I am not, although my present sleepwalking episodes, marked by a tousled blanket on the couch or a water bottle left oddly on the bathroom vanity, are not nearly as dramatic as they were during my single days. Back then, I didn't just sleepwalk, I staged elaborate (albeit unconscious) productions.

Within the walls of my brownstone apartment, I once woke up with a stainless steel bowl full of ice on the floor next to my antique brass bed. That was significantly less inert than the time I woke to find a number of roasted turkey bones (scavenged from the previous night's meal) scattered about me, on which my tomcat was blissfully gnawing away.

My grandest nocturnal production of all time revealed itself as I woke one morning to a strong sweet smell. I lay blinking in bed, traversing the thin plenum that separates awake from asleep, sniffing and sniffing. I recognized the scent but could not place it. There was a trail of clean toilet paper (facial quality Cottonelle, single ply) on the floor next to my bed. It was neatly unrolled all the way out of my bedroom, down the hall and into the den. Along its length was a precisely applied bead of some white, creamy substance.

I followed it until I found the rest of the toilet paper, still on its roll and next to that, my bottle of Finesse hair conditioner. Mystified, I inspected the apartment for clues that might explain the sculpture, but there were none. I disposed of the toilet paper and returned the hair conditioner to its place on the porcelain edge of the tub. Despite my clean-up, the perfumey smell lingered for days.

When I am fully conscious, however, I am not the sort of woman who brings stuffed bears or other items into the bed with me. My Goat and various marital aids are exceptions, as are my rocks.

I procured the rocks during a family vacation in Kentucky, where we were enjoying the Mammoth Cave area. After a day of hearty spelunking, we were en route back to our motel when a billboard steered us to

Kentucky, where we were enjoying the Mammoth Cave area. After a day of hearty spelunking, we were en route back to our motel when a billboard steered us to "Kentucky's Largest Rock Shop." We followed the signs to "Big Mike's" sprawling complex, which included the famed rock shop, a gift and souvenir shop and the tantalizing "Mystery House."

The exterior area in front of the rock shop was lined with rocks. Shiny rocks, glassy rocks, crystalline rocks. All sorts of rocks. Inside were more of the same, only better. There were tiny pouches of rocks, rock jewelry, native crafts, handcrafts, and carved rocks. It went on and on. My kid was drawn to every shimmering object. I walked among the shelves and other tourists, fingering the huge chunks of amethyst and bins of crystals.

"You're one of them," came a voice from behind the counter. I looked up.

"Pardon me?" I said.

"Reiki," she said. She was an attractive woman of some years with a thick pile of blond hair.

"Me?" I said, idiotically bringing my finger to my chest.

"Don't I always spy them?" she said to her assistant.

There were dozens of other patrons milling around the store, yet she was focused solely on me. I was stunned at having been outted as a Reiki practitioner by a complete stranger. It was true; I had taken a Reiki class a few years before when I started suffering from acute panic attacks shortly after my mother's first diagnosis of cancer. I never told anyone about the panic attacks. I told very few people about the Reiki, which did indeed seem to calm them and which I have practiced quietly ever since.

"You practice Reiki, no?" she asked.

"Um," I looked over either shoulder and murmured, "I guess."

"I have something you will like," she said and bustled from behind the counter and into the belly of the laby-rinthine shop. She returned with two smooth egg-shaped stones, each the perfect size to fit in my palms.

"These are Shiva Lingam stones," she said and explained they came from India. She tapped them together and moved them in the space in front of me, explaining their healing and balancing powers.

I liked their easy shape and earthy colors. And they did have an unmistakable energy. These were a pet rocks I could understand.

We purchased the rocks and a pouch of polished gemstones for my daughter. Then we dodged raindrops across the parking lot to the gift shop, where we bought coconut slice candy, a snow dome and a tee shirt, the price of which had been reduced by half on account of a paint stain. The Mystery House, with its tilted rooms, fun house

mirrors and black-lit posters, was worth every penny of the
$1 admission and then some.

That night, I lounged on the motel bed and considered
my new rocks. I tapped them together and moved them
over the swells and swoops of an imaginary rollercoaster in
front of my body. I swished them in circles and spirals with
a flourish. Eventually, I cupped the Shiva Lingam stones in
either palm, curled onto my side and fell fast asleep.

Not long after that, I was sleeping with the rocks
every night. I soon determined the lighter color rock with
the tan "cap" was the girl rock and the darker one was the
boy rock. The girl rock had elaborate markings and was
slightly larger than the boy rock. She fit best in my right
hand, with the boy rock in my left. It didn't feel right to
hold them the other way. The girl rock was more powerful
than the boy rock, a characteristic that endeared her to me
(although I was charmed by the way the boy rock adored
his stronger mate).

I began to believe the rocks had a subtle magic. In
bed, I would place them atop the Goat's back when he was
restless and believe they calmed him, or roll them around
my tummy and giggle, imagining darling little Happy
Earth rays were shooting from the rocks into my beleaguered organs. I liked the way the rocks felt in my hands as
I drifted off to sleep. I imagined they'd make my sleep my
restorative. Perhaps they would even dampen my snoring.

Most of the time I wake up with rocks in hand. Sometimes my splendid king and I are waking up to the sound of one of the rocks hitting the wood floor of our bedroom. If I perchance wake up in the normal course of my strange nocturnal behavior and find I am no longer clutching the rocks, I grope around and usually find them right next to me. If not, I search under the blankets and pillows (I sleep with a minimum of three arranged around my body in an indulgent U; the Goat gets one pillow and grudgingly at that).

On occasion, I cannot find a rock. Then I turn my attention to the soundly sleeping Goat, who is invariably on his stomach. As soon as my probing fingers slide beneath his furry torso, however, something happens. His right hand–and only his right hand–slowly goes into motion and produces the rock from underneath his corpse-like body. The hand pushes it over to me and returns to its position over the Goat's head. Wordlessly, I scoop up the rock and scuttle back over to my side of the bed, where I burrow into my pillow nest and fall back to sleep, rocks safely in hand.

When I have to turn on the light in order to find a rock, that will usually rouse the Goat. He will roll over and blink at me and the offending light.

"Where's my rock?" I will say indignantly, implying that said loss is entirely his fault.

The Goat of course deserves none of this and is indulgent to a fault concerning my nightly shenanigans. When my heroic snoring ensues, he eases me onto my side as if I am a delicate pastry dough. If that doesn't do the trick he waits and tries again. Or he'll find my magic rocks and place them near my hands. And if that doesn't work, he gives up and buries himself beneath his pillow.

Snoring, rock husbandry and unconscious hair product/toilet paper crafting does not conclude the trials of sleeping with Erin.

The muse will often visit me at night. She is a terrible Disneyesque Medusa, towering above my bed as I quake beneath the covers, peering up at her like Scrooge before the Ghost of Christmas Yet to Come.

"You must improve the barroom scene!" she might demand of a piece of fiction, or "The entire introduction is expository!" might be her commentary on a short essay. She sneers and rages until I get out of bed, or will nibble and bite at my toes if the complaints are not enough.

Eventually, I leave my sleeping husband and slink into my office in the spare bedroom.

As is widely known, the temperature in Cleveland, Ohio is not moderate for several months out of the year. The proper technical term for the Cleveland air on a standard January night is "colder than a brass monkey's pecker." Most Clevelanders compensate the frigid temperatures by setting their thermostats to 68 degrees Fahrenheit or (gasp!) even higher.

Not me (and I am purposefully engaging the singular, for the following is strictly an Erin mandate). Our thermostat is set to 64 degrees Fahrenheit from 7 a.m. to 10 p.m. and 62 degrees during all other hours (this is a softening of the previous temperature guidelines of 62/55 that ruled prior to the installation of our high efficiency furnace). Hence, when I rise to attend the demands of the terrifying muse and commit fingertips to keyboard, it can be COLD.

I always tell myself that I'll just jot a few notes, that it will take just a minute, and that the donning of slippers and proper clothing is not necessary. A "few notes" quickly expands into a complete thought and an associated sentence or two, which grows into a paragraph and so on. If it's cold enough, I will sometimes drape a blanket around the computer and myself, turning the whole operation into a ghostly tent from whence the tappity-tap on the keys and my low nonsensical commentary emanate.

"a fra- fra- fra ... hmmmm."

Eventually, my body unleashes a dose of melatonin that I sense as acutely as an injection of opium and the need for sleep is upon me. Blanket tent notwithstanding, I am frozen solid by this time, particularly my feet. I creep back into the bedroom, wherein my dearly beloved is breathing evenly and deeply beneath his sea of blankets, aptly insulated against the cold night.

The rest of the story is obvious enough, but earns it's telling by way of my sheer relishing of the moment. On those cold winter nights, I do not slip between the covers and slowly inch over to enjoy the outer rings of my husband's warm spot, then insinuate myself closer and closer to his delicious heat.

No, no, no.

Stripped of the distraction of my writing, my frozen fingers and feet garner all of my attention. I dive into the bed and, cold as an icicle, immediately wrap myself around my toasty spouse, seeking out the warmest crevices on him, into which I nuzzle the coldest bits of me.

To assuage my guilt at such moments, I like to think of my husband as the Marc Antony character in the Warner Bros. classic cartoon *Feed the Kitty*, in which a big gruff bulldog (Marc Antony) cares for a tiny kitty. As indicated by beads of sweat popping from his forehead, Marc Antony silently endures the pain of the kitty's clawing and preening upon his fleshy back in order to relish the darling moment when the kitty, finally nestled in the bulldog's fur, falls asleep and purrs.

File that one next to Sleeping Erin–only in my dreams.

###

As with most people, my dreams disappear as quickly as a beer foam mustache. But there are those that stick. Some linger for just a few hours, others I remember for years. The nightmare in which I am walking through a brightly lit grocery only to find the butcher slicing a live man's head in the rear of the store has been with me longer than my husband, as has the feeling of being flattened by a steamroller, a scene which played out in another dream when I was a child. I blinked awake just as the black steel roller overtook me, wondering if I was still alive and glad that it hadn't hurt too much. Another dream had me gazing at my knee, only to find a perfectly formed mouth upon it. The lips moved and stretched against the white white teeth. There was no tongue.

Growing up amid the hunkering industrial backdrop of Cleveland lent itself to countless dreams of floundering in the murky Cuyahoga River among the huge bridge pilings. Once I woke relieved to discover that, no, I was not inside the cargo hold of a massive ore freighter, but neatly contained in my comfy bed. When my brother John or Dad visits my dreams, they are always disappointed in me. Or leaving me. Or returning to me reluctantly.

Happier dreams have me flying or running through air so clean it has a smell. My favorite dream featured a blue sea in which VW Beetles, the colors of Necco Wafers, floated about. The people inside the jolly round cars were laughing and laughing and laughing.

Some dreams have me wake repeating senseless refrains (*levee over the green, levee over the green*), wondering over their secret message. Others feature decaying corpses in hidden rooms of baroque mansions where they wait for me.

Then there are the sex dreams.

For a married woman, there are few gifts as well earned as dreams of filthy carnal indulgences with exotic men. In the boudoir of my mind, I can embark on a voyage of dripping pleasure at the hands of Quint, Randall McMurphy or Lewis Medlock, without one shred of guilt. Here I am blameless to a fault; fast asleep, not even consciously choosing the lascivious acts. I'm free to enjoy every probe, push, thrust and squeeze without condemnation. As long as I'm asleep, can it even be categorized as lusting of the heart? Surely not! After all, the dreams come to me; I do not come to the dreams. I am at their mercy (perhaps courtesy of a silken coil of rope draped invitingly over the bare shoulder of [gasp] Mike Rowe).

If only that were the case.

Sadly, instead of Vincent D'Onofrio or Rally Caparas or that one guy who works at the place where I take my car for new tires whose name-patch says "Rick," I get face-less men, the occasional woman or weird amalgams such as my high school Civics teacher's head on my high school boyfriend's body.

Then there is the pinnacle of sex dream injustices: the exquisite reverie that features (gulp) my husband. When I rouse from the heady image of a warm wet mouth only to realize that it's the mouth I can have pretty much any time I want, resentment blooms. I've been cheated and someone needs to pay. Conveniently, he who is easiest to blame is usually sound asleep right next to me.

Using my thumb to spring load my forefinger, I'll flick my husband sharply on the forehead. He'll startle, then blink awake to see me propped up on one elbow, looking back at him with irritation.

"What?" he'll say.

"Goddamnit!" I'll say.

"What did I do?" he says.

"Goddamnit!" I flick his forehead again.

"What!?"

"I just had a really good sex dream with like … " I stammer, "… really good…sex stuff in it!"

"Congratulations," he says, fumbling for his glasses.

"Shall I call the NewsNet 5 tipline?"

"I hardly think so," I say. "You were in it. It was you and me."

"So?"

"So!" I say. "It's my dirty dream. Don't you think I deserve to have sex with, say … " I have to stop to think, my eyes fluttering as if I have a scant handful of seconds to select a chocolate from an irresistible collection, " … Jim Cantore?"

"Which one is he again?"

"The weather channel guy," I say, "And shouldn't I be entitled to sex with him—at least in my dreams—after dealing with your filthy member for all these years?"

"My filthy member?" he says.

"That's right," I say while admitting to myself that even when I am fully awake and enjoying a fantasy of my own construct, I may choose different players, but in the end, their ministrations always mimic that of my husband. I truly cannot escape him. "Who dreams of sex with their husband?" I ask defiantly.

"You," he says with smug satisfaction

"Goddamn it, Nowjack! You miserable Goat!" I say. "You warlock!"

He whom I have and hold removes his glasses.

"Casting spells on poor defenseless sleeping women in the middle of the night!"

My splendid king moves over to my side of the bed.

"Goddamnit," I say again, more half-heartedly. "What are you doing over here," but it's not really a question. "Hey. No," I protest weakly. "Get back over there," I say. "Don't."

He does anyway.

"Filthy oinking ... " I intend to add "goat," but the word clogs in my throat, then dissolves into a raspy purr.

Water

It is late afternoon, June 22, 2006.

It's raining. The neighbor kids are over playing with my daughter downstairs. It's my husband's day off. I am at work at the computer.

Next to my elbow is an invitation to play Bunco later in the week. "Bring ten bucks and a boobie prize," it says. One of the women on my street organized this inaugural Bunco gathering and promised us all that it's a simple dice game anyone can play. The theme is "summer fun."

The women in my neighborhood are of a certain ilk. They have been married forever, buy toilet paper on sale, and given twenty minutes and a can of Campbell's soup, they can produce something that looks like dinner. They understand how the cries of pleasure during climax are tethered to the cries of pain during childbirth. These are the women you call in an emergency.

They also know how to laugh hard and that a good long marriage depends on good long sex. When the power goes out for three days, they figure out a way to keep the beer cold and the milk fresh.

I do not go to church. I drink and swear too much. I have a tattoo. Despite all of this and the fact that I lean left while most of them lean right, I am tolerated by the women in my neighborhood—more than tolerated. They invite me to every barbecue and cocktail party. They even hosted a party for me when my humble novel debuted. To be counted among the women in my neighborhood is no small honor to me.

They include me either because I am funny or perhaps because I've been around so long I've earned squatter's rights. Whatever the reason, I fully intend to become a part of this collective Bunco movement.

Bored with my work, I poke around the Internet with silly "Bunco" queries. As I peruse the scant Wiki entry for the game, the rain intensifies and the sky darkens. A bolt of lightning flashes as thunder booms in the distance. I groan, knowing I should shut down the computer. The rain beats against my office window and streams down the glass.

Water, I think.

As the sound of the storm escalates and the sunlight all but disappears, a switch somewhere inside of me toggles from off to on. I go downstairs and check the sunken door well that is outside of the family room. Water is beginning to pool in it.

"Honey?" I say to my husband, "The door drain is

clogged again," because if the door well drain is clogged and it rains long and hard enough, the water will come in beneath the door and soak the living room carpet, it's happened once before. We know the door is a flooding hazard and needs to be removed. We just haven't gotten that far yet.

Eric heaves himself from the couch. I go out to the garage, push a button and the garage door responds, rumbling open to expose an unobstructed view of my environs.

My eyes open wide. Expletives fall from beneath my breath as I try to process what is before me: a solid sheet of rain, roiling torrents, and familiar houses.

"Drain's clear," says Eric as he steps up behind me. "Just too much water coming down too fast for it to keep up," Then he sees the newborn rivers that are flowing around our neighbor's house and down the street. They are filling a lake that is not supposed to be there.

I drink water. I bathe in water.

I run back inside to find water just beginning to seep in under the door.

"You kids get me some towels," I say. They do and I peel back the carpet and shove them around the base of the door.

"Don't you kids set one foot out of this house," I say. They nod silently with the clear-eyed expressions of children who know something larger is at work. "Not one foot," I repeat before heading back outside. Their frantic whispers ensue as soon as my back is turned.

And the water is pouring in from the stubbed dead-end of the street. And the water is coming from the new development behind our house. And the water is coming from the retention basin across the street. And it is shooting up from the storm drains and making white crests as it whorls over itself. It moves like a living thing.

My body is 75 percent water.

The lake that is not supposed to be there is getting larger and is now so deep that only the cheery red tip of the fire hydrant breaks its surface.

I cannot survive more than four or five days without water.

I step from beneath the protection of my garage roof. The street is not a street anymore. It is a river. The rain pummels down as I approach my neighbor, whose home is now completely surrounded in water. We are both soaking wet. My neighbor is holding a hoe and we are looking at the impossible water.

"Goddamn," I say.

My neighbor's wife yells out to him and although neither of us can hear her words over the rain and the raging torrents and the thunder, her waving arms garner our attention. Her husband runs to her.

I turn back to my own house. Eric walks from behind it in a dripping yellow slicker. He is poking yard drains with a rake.

The cheery red top of the fire hydrant, which supplies water in case of fire, is no longer visible. The smell coming from the floodwater is suspect and the words *e coli* race through my mind. The kids, curious and excited and frightened, tiptoe from the house. Their umbrellas are the colors of m&m's.

"You kids get back in that house now!" I scream. "No discussion!" *E coli. Downed wires.*

I wade through the brown water, making my way up the street. People are emerging from their houses. Susan stands defiantly framed by her open front door as she watches the water rise higher and higher according to her mailbox. She's holding a broom.

The rain slacks off, but the water continues to swell. The lake that is not supposed to be there eventually reaches a depth of three and a half feet. Another neighbor comes home from work, parks at the edge of the lake that now covers our street and trudges through the water to his home.

Although I know this experience pales in comparison, the next time a newscaster utters the words tsunami or hurricane, something inside me will click and I will remember this water on this day.

I stand with my neighbors, murmuring and shaking my head along with them, my arms crossed over my chest. Within a ten mile radius, half of a local lumber yard that has been in business since 1947 falls into an adjacent creek; human waste fills over a hundred basements; and cars float like corks in a submerged parking lot.

An hour, another hour, another hour. Still, our street is impassable.

The 50-foot high white petroleum storage tanks my husband services as he wears a shirt with a name patch are anchored to the earth with massive steel chains. The tanks are adjacent to the Cuyahoga River, within the floodplain. They hold diesel fuel, which is lighter than water. During the frequent floods, the tanks would float if not secured. And if my husband were ever to fall into one of the massive vessels, he would sink to the bottom and die. Human beings, composed chiefly of water, cannot swim or float in diesel fuel.

When I return home, I find only a few wet towels at the base of the problematic door. The concept of *thankful* blossoms inside of me. The longest day of the year dissolves into night.

I gather up my $10 and "summer fun" booby prize

(a jar of gourmet BBQ sauce) and head to Jane's house to play Bunco. I walk by unnatural groupings of waterlogged upholstered chairs and upended tables on lawns and driveways. There are piles of ruined boxed games: Scrabble and Risk and Clue. Rolls of sodden carpet line the street along with shorted-out joysticks and printers and rec room televisions.

An unfamiliar van drives away with its unhappy promises: 24-HOUR WATER EXTRACTION, WATER AND SEWAGE DAMAGE, DRYING AND DEHUMIDIFYING.

At Jane's place, I step upon the stone tile in the front foyer that is exactly the same as the stone tile in my own foyer and make my way into the kitchen where I join the group and nosh chips and quaff beer and sangria while we wait for Susan.

"Where the hell is Sue?"

"She's not doing her hair, is she? Tell me she is not doing her hair."

The women in my neighborhood are in tee shirts and shorts and ponytails. They are discussing upcoming summer sporting events and family gatherings. No one is complaining.

"Christ, Erin finished her beer already."

Susan finally shows up with perfect hair and lipstick, a warm cherry cobbler in her oven-mitted hands.

"Susan, you are wearing lipstick."

When my father died, the women in my neighborhood brought baked ham for my family and me. They brought warm covered dishes carried in oven-mitted hands. They offered to do anything to help out. And they meant it.

Mary, who knows a thing or two about salvaging waterlogged baby pictures, comments on Sue's makeup as well as her own. "You? Look at you! Me? I just did a resurface."

The Bunco game begins. The game is played in rounds with rotating partners. I lose the first couple of rounds.

"Somebody get Erin another beer."

"Erin lost again."

"I'm staying at the 'loser' table on purpose," I say. "It's close to the beer."

I lose the next couple of rounds.

"Did Erin lose again?"

"What do you think?"

I lose some more. The cherry cobbler is warm and rich and buttery.

"Erin's never going to sit at the winners' table."

I lose every single round.

"Ladies, this is not losing," I say. "This was my plan all along. Have you any idea the practice I've put into this?" I pick up a trio of dice and roll them with a flourish.

As the biggest loser of the night, I am the recipient

of all the boobie prizes (heart-shaped sunglasses, scented votive candles, boxes of sparklers, plastic hors d'oeuvre forks with star-shaped handles).

"Who's going to help Erin carry all this crap home?"

We say our thankyous and vow to do it again the following month. Then, the women in my neighborhood walk down our street, passing the piles of waterlogged debris once again.

The next day I open the front door to a spectacular morning and a surprise. Under the cloak of night, my gambling buddies have copiously noted my staggering Bunco loss on the surface of our drive.

"BUNCO LOSER" in white chalk, "BIGGEST LOSER" in pink and "ERIN CAN'T ROLL" in blue.

I step over the letters on my way to the newspaper box, as laughter begins rumbling from deep in my belly. It wells up through me until tears squeeze from my eyes. A bird glides overhead.

"NO BUNCO HERE!"

Due north, the sun dapples Lake Erie with a web of glittering diamonds. On the other side of the earth, lovers languish beneath the moon. Due south, a frail man sees his last vision of life as a newborn baby's eyes open for the first time. Blood flows. Blood spills. Blood dries.

I face east and inhale, turn to the west and exhale. I step over my threshold and into the rest of my life.